Jewish Holidays Cookbook

Jewish Holidays
Cookbook

Festive meals for celebrating the year

by Jill Colella Bloomfield

Rabbi Janet Ozur Bass, consultant
photography by Angela Coppola

DK | Penguin Random House

Editor	Nancy Ellwood
Designer	Bill Miller
Managing Art Editor	Michelle Baxter
Art Director	Dirk Kaufman
DTP Coordinator	Kathy Farias
Pre-Production Producer	Dragana Puvacic
Producer	John Casey
Publishing Director	Beth Sutinis

Photography by Angela Coppola

This paperback edition published, 2018
First edition, 2008
Published in the United States by DK Publishing
345 Hudson Street, New York, New York 10014

Copyright © 2008, 2018 Dorling Kindersley Limited
DK, a Division of Penguin Random House LLC
18 19 20 21 10 9 8 7 6 5 4 3 2 1
001-JD086-May/2018

A catalog record for this book is available from
the Library of Congress.
ISBN 978-1-4654-7825-2

DK books are available at special discounts
for bulk purchases for sales promotions, premiums,
fund-raising, or educational use.
For details, contact:
DK Publishing Special Markets,
345 Hudson Street, New York, NY 10014
SpecialSales@dk.com

Color Reproduction by Colourscan, Singapore
Printed and bound in China

A WORLD OF IDEAS:
SEE ALL THERE IS TO KNOW

www.dk.com

contents

16 Shabbat

Challah • Roasted Chicken with Vegetables • Chicken Noodle Soup Matzoh Balls • Vegetable Cholent • Chickpea and Couscous Salad

30 Rosh Hashanah

Sweet Ginger Gefilte Fish • Soda Pop Brisket • Sweet Carrot Tzimmes • Harvest Rice with Pomegranate Seeds • Sweet Potato Casserole • Honey Lemon Cake

44 Yom Kippur

Bagels with Cream Cheese • Smoked Salmon Frittata • Basic Any-Which-Way Kugel • Mandel Bread

foreword

The Jewish holidays teach us that there are many ways and many places to celebrate Jewish tradition. As a rabbi I meet many people who think that the synagogue is the center of Jewish life, and it is indeed a very important place for the Jewish community to gather. However, as a mother and a daughter, I know that the home—and table—is the centerpiece where families can find, create, and pass down tradition.

Cooking with people we care about allows us a way to share memories and create new ones. Most people can remember the smell of their favorite food from childhood, or a kind word that was passed along with a great taste. Both the word and the taste enhance each other.

My mother taught me many important lessons in the kitchen. She taught me that Friday night is a sacred time for family, and always added a little more love to her Shabbat recipes. And she taught me that food is an important way to remember the people we love when she showed me how her mother made the foods that she loved while growing up.

My memories of our Jewish kitchen are filled with the hilarious laughter and beautiful music of my mother, my sisters, and all the wonderful people who came into our lives. The food, while it tasted terrific on the table, somehow tasted like magic when we were all together in the kitchen preparing it. We created our "sister assembly lines" to make Purim hamantaschen, Shabbat challah, and matzoh balls. Whether I was rolling, cutting, kneading, filling, or pinching, my sisters and I were side by side celebrating what it means to be Jewish.

We should all grab a pot, a pan, some ingredients, and this idea: We can teach valuable Jewish lessons in our kitchens and at our dining room tables. We can teach someone that cooking is about using our resources wisely, being generous, and taking only what we need. We can teach the mitzvah of hospitality by graciously opening our hearts and homes to old friends and family, and extend that mitzvah to new friends who might have no other holiday table at which to celebrate.

When we put care and love into the food we create for the Jewish holidays, we, too, can become a part of the amazing legacy of the Jewish tradition.

Janet J Bass

how to use this book

Welcome to *Jewish Holidays Cookbook*! Inside you'll not only learn to cook traditional Jewish foods, but you'll learn about why those foods are important to Jewish culture, and why people eat them for certain holidays. There is a lot of information coming your way, so here's a look at what the pages ahead mean.

PESACH

Pesach brings families together to the seder table in celebration of their history and traditions. It is a time to remember the struggles of the Israelites, and to eat and enjoy matzoh, haroset, meringues, and other treats from the Old World.

Pesach, or Passover, celebrates the trials and triumphs of the Israelite people in Egypt.

Pharaoh kept the Israelites as slaves, and treated them cruelly for many years. When he finally decided to let the Israelites follow Moses out of Egypt, the Israelites left in a hurry because they feared that Pharaoh would change his mind. He did change his mind, and sent his army after them. So the Israelites fled into the desert.

Because they left Egypt so quickly, the Israelites did not have time to let their bread dough rise before baking it. So instead of having leavened bread, they had flat matzoh. To remember the escape of Israelite ancestors, many Jews do not eat leavened foods during Pesach. Some families completely remove anything that contains flour or leavening agents (called "*chametz*") from their homes during Pesach.

Seder plate

"The Torah teaches that the first seder was held the night before the Israelites left Egypt. They ate Passover lamb and talked about the miracles that were happening all around them."

–Rabbi Ozur Bass

During the first two nights of Pesach, a seder is held, at which the Haggadah is read aloud. *Haggadah* means "the telling," and it tells the story of the Israelites' flight from Egypt.

Everything on the seder table is used to help tell the story, especially the items placed on the special seder plate. The symbolic foods on the seder plate are: a roasted shank bone, a roasted egg, horseradish, romaine lettuce (or parsley), celery, and haroset.

After the Haggadah is read, families celebrate with a delicious, festive meal. Many of the dishes traditionally served hearken back to ancient times, and are based on the foods available to the Israelites as they continued their journey through the desert.

Meringue cookies are perfect for Pesach.

the chapters

Each major holiday has its own chapter in the book. Each chapter starts with an introduction that tells you a bit about that holiday, its history and traditions, and how food plays a role.

the recipes

Rabbi Ozur Bass tells us about her cooking experiences throughout the years.

This color bar will tell you in which season each holiday takes place. (This one's fall)

These food tips give you a little more info on the recipe itself.

This tells you how many people each recipe serves.

Some recipes have variations that you can try.

Here's a list of the foods you'll need to make the recipe.

This tells you which holiday you're cooking for.

Learn a bit about the recipe and the holiday.

These are the instructions that tell you how to make the recipe.

Step-by-step photos will help you along.

Look here for extra tips and information.

Want to know if a recipe is dairy, meat, or pareve? Find it here.

Final pictures show you how the recipe should look when it's complete.

basic any-which-way kugel

Kugel is a baked egg-and-noodle dish that can be sweet or savory. Everyone has his or her favorite ingredients. With this recipe, you can make one delicious kugel or custom-make mini kugels to suit everyone's tastes!

"Kugel is one of the most popular and well-known Jewish foods. When it has dried fruit in it, it is called *Yerushalmi*, which means 'from Jerusalem.'" –Rabbi Ozur Bass

raspberry ponchik

Polish ponchik are fried doughnuts stuffed with jelly. Eastern European Jews brought these with them as they moved to Israel. This quick and easy recipe allows anyone to celebrate Hanukkah with homemade jelly doughnuts.

cooking tools

When you go to school you need notebooks and pencils and folders. When you cook, you need similar tools of the trade. Chances are you've got everything you need right in your kitchen. See below for a list of kitchen tools and appliances that will come in handy when preparing your recipes.

Baking sheet

Also called a cookie sheet. This is a flat baking pan with no raised edges. Baking sheets should be used only for cookies and breads that will not spread very much when they bake.

Colander

Used to drain water from ingredients such as pasta or egg noodles. Colanders are also perfect for rinsing off fresh fruits and vegetables.

Cookie cutters

These forms are used to cut dough, sandwiches, or any soft food into fun shapes. Cookie cutters come in thousands of sizes and styles.

Cutting board

A surface upon which all ingredients should be cut. Some cutting boards are made of wood, others of plastic. It's a good idea to have separate cutting boards for raw meats, raw fish, and fresh fruits and vegetables.

Deep-frying thermometer

Used to measure the temperature of oil for frying.

Electric mixer

Used to mix just about anything. Electric mixers can be standing (such as this one), or handheld, and have different attachments for mixing different types of ingredients.

Frying pan

Also called a skillet. This is a large, flat pan on which foods cook evenly because they can be spread out into one layer.

Grater

This is used to shred ingredients such as cheese, potatoes, onions, and carrots.

Jelly roll pan

A flat baking pan with raised edges so that batter will stay in the pan. Often used to make thin, flat cakes.

Measuring cups

Used to measure out the exact amount of each ingredient.

Meat thermometer

Used to measure the internal temperature of meats such as beef, chicken, and lamb.

Microplane

This is a very fine grater, used to scrape the zest off of oranges, lemons, and limes.

Oven mitts

These protect your hands from hot pots and pans. Be sure they're clean and dry when you use them.

Parchment paper

This paper is often used to line baking sheets or cake pans to prevent food from sticking to the pan. It is also used to create packets in which food is steamed (called "en papillote").

Rolling pin

Used to roll out dough for cookies and pies. Can also be used to crush crackers, cookies, or cornflakes into crumbs.

Saucepan

A deep pot used to cook liquids and stews, and to boil pasta, noodles, rice, and couscous.

Skewers

Used to make kebabs. Skewers are often made of bamboo or metal. Bamboo skewers work best if they are soaked in cold water for about an hour before you use them (this prevents them from catching fire while on a grill).

Spatula

There are two types of spatulas: rubber spatulas help scrape food and batter from bowls. Flat spatulas are used to scoop food up off a pan or cooking surface.

Springform pan

A metal baking pan whose sides are removable. They can be expanded by opening the metal latch and then lifted away while delicate cakes (such as cheesecake) remain on the metal base.

Tongs

Used to grab large ingredients while they're cooking. You can use tongs to turn food in a pan.

Whisk

Used to whip food to a light, airy consistency.

Wooden spoons

Used to stir just about anything. Wooden spoons are great because they don't get hot like metals spoons do.

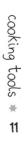

kitchen safety

Working in the kitchen is an enjoyable experience, especially if you follow some important guidelines: Be sure to closely review your recipe before you start. Make sure you have the proper tools. And be safe! Clear off your work space, take your time, be careful, and always ask an adult for help when you need it. Here are some more guidelines to follow as you whip your recipes into shape:

- ### Permission, please

  Always ask an adult's permission before you begin to cook. Know—and follow—the rules of your kitchen, and if you need help, ask for it.

- ### Avoid accidents

  To avoid kitchen mishaps, get ready for cooking before you begin. Roll up long sleeves. Tie back long hair. Know how to use a kitchen fire extinguisher. Clean up spills as soon as they occur so no one slips and falls. For dangerous accidents like broken glass, ask an adult for help.

- ### Hot pots

  Be careful of hot pots and pans. Be sure to have plenty of clean, dry pot holders and oven mitts to protect your hands. Don't substitute a dish towel for a pot holder.

- ### Wash up and keep clean

  Always wash your hands before handling food. Once your hands are clean, avoid touching your hair and face. Any time you sneeze, use the bathroom, or touch raw meats, go ahead and wash your hands again.

- ### Handling food wisely

  Be sure to use clean utensils and cutting boards. Wash fruit and vegetables carefully to remove dirt and sand. Always wash your hands immediately after handling raw meat, chicken, fish, and eggs. If any juices from raw meat spill, wipe them up right away. It's a good idea to use different cutting boards for raw meats, raw fish, and fruits and veggies.

- ### Knife know-how

  Always ask an adult for help when using sharp knives. Use the smallest knife you need to do the job. Be sure to keep your fingers away from sharp blades. Never leave a knife hanging off the edge of the counter. And never put a knife in a place where someone can't see it, like in a sink filled with soapy water.

Don't lick your fingers while you cook.

Wash your hands after handling raw eggs.

keeping kosher

The word *kosher* means "fit or proper for use." Kosher cooking involves foods—and the utensils used to cook the foods—that are prepared a certain way, and deemed fit and proper for eating. The laws that govern this are called the laws of kashrut.

The laws of kashrut come from two main sources: the Torah and rabbinic law. The Torah gives many laws about which animals Jews can eat, and which they cannot. Some of these laws state that Jews can eat only land mammals that chew their cud and have true, split hooves (like cows), or sea animals that have both fins and scales (like most fish). Animals forbidden by the Torah include pigs, snakes and reptiles, some birds, and sea animals that have hard shells (like lobsters and crabs).

Rabbinic law is the second source of kosher rules, and often expands on laws introduced in the Torah. Where the Torah says that a goat may not be cooked in its mother's milk, rabbinic law states that no meat product of any kind may be cooked, prepared, or eaten with any dairy product. Rabbinic law also teaches that for an animal to be kosher it must be slaughtered and prepared in a particular way.

Besides being meat or dairy, kosher foods can also be pareve (pronounced *PARV*). Pareve foods have neither meat nor dairy in them, and therefore can be eaten with both. Fruits, vegetables, eggs, fish, and grains are all pareve.

The laws of kashrut may seem complicated, but it is not that difficult to keep a kosher kitchen. Most people will separate utensils, dishes, and cooking areas in which to prepare meat and dairy foods. Mass-produced foods (like cereals and snacks that you buy at the store) are marked with special symbols to indicate that they are kosher.

Neither the Torah nor rabbinic law explain *why* kosher rules were given, although throughout history many people have tried to come up with explanations.

Most people follow the laws of kashrut because they believe that keeping these rules is an important part of being Jewish, and because they believe this is what God would like them to do. Even so, the decision to keep kosher is a very personal one, often handed down through families from generation to generation.

No matter whether it's kosher or not, food plays an important role in Jewish culture. The recipes in this cookbook are based on many traditional foods cooked throughout the world, some with a modern twist. There are many more recipes still out there to be explored! Please note that none of the recipes here are specifically kosher, but they are labeled "meat," "dairy," or "pareve." Simple variations are offered so that you can maintain a kosher meal.

introduction

Food is a very important part of our lives. We need it to survive, of course, but we also use it to express our cultural identity. What we eat at home is a statement about where we are raised, what foods are available, and what flavors our parents hand down to us. And every year we have many opportunities to celebrate our culture and our history through food, especially during our holidays!

What we decide to eat depends on many factors—what foods are in season, what foods are familiar to us, and what holiday we are celebrating. Beginning with recipes for Shabbat such as challah, roasted chicken, and matzoh balls, this book explores Jewish holidays and festivals through delicious recipes.

Different festivals and holidays have special foods associated with them. The Jewish year begins at Rosh Hashanah, and recipes to welcome a sweet new year include sweet-and-sour gefilte fish, soda pop brisket, and honey cake. At Yom Kippur, after a meaningful fast, try recipes for kugel and smoked salmon frittata at your family's break-the-fast party.

Because Hanukkah is a time to remember the miracle of oil, its traditional foods are fried, like crispy potato latkes and *sufganiyot*. After Hanukkah, celebrate Tu B'Shevat—the festival of trees—by cooking with fruits and nuts. Fig spread and Tu B'Shevat granola are fun to eat in the shade of a beautiful old tree.

Purim can be made merry with hamantaschen and other recipes. The Achashverosh crown sandwich is easy (and tasty) to eat when hurrying to a Purim carnival.

Pesach, or Passover, is a time when cooks must be innovative as they avoid using leavening ingredients such as flour. Recipes like an Israeli meat pie called *mina* are easy to make. And flourless meringues are a great dessert at a seder.

Middle Eastern flavors influence Yom Ha'Atzmaut recipes like Israeli salad, falafel, and hummus, which are festive treats for celebrating independence.

Lag B'Omer is for picnics, bonfires, and recipes for lamb shish kebab, watermelon salad, and pomegranate lemonade. Shavuot is a holiday that celebrates the bounty of the spring harvest and receiving the Torah. Rich dairy foods like blintzes and cheesecake make Shavuot delicious to observe.

At the end you'll find pages on which you can take notes about the recipes. Record any variations or special touches that you've made to your dishes.

No matter if you're a beginning chef or already a pro in the kitchen, cooking new recipes is a wonderful way to celebrate the holidays. And if your dishes don't turn out perfectly, don't worry. Experimenting and trying again are all part of the cooking adventure. So invite your family and friends—Jewish and non-Jewish—into the kitchen to experience with you the delicious and diverse Jewish year!

Jill Bloomfield

How many ways can you cook with matzoh?

SHABBAT

How wonderfully special it is to be Jewish! Each week has its own joyful celebration. Every Friday at sundown Shabbat begins. Special candles are lit and a prayer is said. Parents bless their children and each other.

Shabbat is a holy day that celebrates God's day of rest after creating the world. On Shabbat, we, too, have the chance to sit back and celebrate all that we have created during the week. It is a special time to share with family and friends, attend services, and relax at home. Shabbat ends on Saturday evening after sundown.

Food is an important part of celebrating Shabbat. Some people say that eating three full meals on Shabbat is a mitzvah. Some people define mitzvahs (or mitzvot) as commandments, meaning that they are something that the Jewish people have to do because God told them to. Other people define mitzvot as traditions that have been kept in the Jewish community for many years. Still others define mitzvot as good deeds, because they believe that God wants them to make the world a better place. However you define mitzvot, they help people understand how we should act toward ourselves, one another, and God. Shabbat is a weekly reminder of the importance of mitzvot.

kiddush cup

"The Jewish faith is one not only of belief, but also of action. We try to act a certain way in this world because of our belief in what it means to be Jewish. Mitzvot help us understand that."
—Rabbi Ozur Bass

Some people make Shabbat a time to focus on family, their friends, and their relationship with God. Because of this they do not drive, watch television, or do homework on Shabbat. Instead, Shabbat is a time to play outside, go to the synagogue to sing and pray, hang out with people you enjoy, or read books just for pleasure.

For some Jews, certain types of work are not allowed on Shabbat, so food must be cooked in advance. Some foods are even left to cook overnight and then eaten the next day. These recipes can become part of your own family traditions.

The *motzi* is said over the challah at Shabbat dinner.

challah

serves
24

Challah is traditionally served at the beginning of Shabbat dinner. A prayer is said over the freshly baked bread before dinner begins. Here's a recipe for your very own special Shabbat challah. This recipe makes two loaves.

get cooking...

1 Pour water into bottom of large mixing bowl. Add yeast, and allow to sit for 1 minute.

2 Add honey, oil, eggs, sugar, and salt to yeast mixture. Stir to combine.

3 Scoop spoonfuls of flour into the wet mixture, combining well each time. As you continue adding flour, the mixture will thicken. You can use your hands to mix in the flour.

4 After all of the flour is mixed in, knead the dough in the bowl until it is smooth. Add up to ½ cup of additional flour if your dough is sticky. Allow dough to rise for 1 hour in a warm place. The dough should double in size.

5 Turn the dough out onto a floured surface like a cutting board. Deflate risen dough by punching it. Divide dough into 2 equal pieces and knead each piece for 3 minutes. If dough is sticky, add a little bit of flour as you knead.

6 Grease 2 large baking sheets with margarine, and set them aside. Preheat the oven to 375°F (190°C).

7 Divide each loaf into 3 equal pieces. Roll each piece into a long rope about 1½ inches (4 cm) in diameter. These will be the 3 strands of your braid. Bring the ends of the strands together and begin braiding. After it is fully braided, tuck the beginning and end of your braid under the loaf. Repeat for the other loaf, and place each on a prepared baking sheet. Cover each loaf with a slightly damp towel and allow the loaves to rise once more, for 45 minutes.

ingredients...

2½ cups warm water

1 tablespoon active dry yeast

½ cup honey

6 tablespoons vegetable oil

2 eggs

1 tablespoon sugar

1 tablespoon salt

8 cups all-purpose flour

1 egg, beaten

2 tablespoons sesame seeds

8 After the loaves have risen, use a pastry brush to spread beaten egg over each one. Sprinkle the tops of the loaves with sesame seeds.

9 Bake on a low rack for about 35 to 45 minutes. The fully baked bread should be a deep golden color and should sound hollow when tapped.

Keep a bowl of flour handy.

Your challah is ready!

Try sprinkling your challah with poppy seeds.

This recipe is pareve. For a kosher meal, you can serve this with either dairy or meat foods.

The plural of challah is "challot."

roasted chicken with vegetables

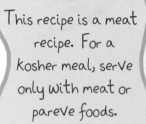

serves
6

Celebrate with a classic Shabbat dinner of roasted chicken and hearty vegetables. Be sure to check that your chicken is fully cooked before serving.

ingredients...

1 whole chicken, about 4 lbs (1.8 kg)

1 tablespoon olive oil

1 teaspoon salt

1 teaspoon pepper

4 cups potato, cut into 2-inch (5-cm) chunks

1 cup onion, chopped

2 cups carrot, cut into 2-inch (5-cm) chunks

1 cup celery, cut into 1-inch (2.5-cm) chunks

1 cup chicken broth

1 teaspoon garlic powder

This recipe is a meat recipe. For a Kosher meal, serve only with meat or pareve foods.

get cooking...

1 Preheat oven to 350°F (180°C). Rinse chicken and pat dry.

2 Rub chicken with olive oil, then sprinkle with salt and pepper. Put in a large roasting pan.

3 Place potatoes under the chicken and arrange other vegetables around the chicken.

4 Add chicken broth to roasting pan, making sure that all vegetables are moistened.

5 Sprinkle vegetables with garlic powder.

6 Cover the chicken and roasting pan tightly with aluminum foil.

7 Roast chicken for 90 minutes, basting occasionally. Then remove foil and roast for 20 minutes at 450°F (230°C) to crisp the skin. The chicken is done when its juices are clear.

Mom or dad can carve the chicken.

"Growing up, my sisters and I could count on the same delicious Shabbat dinner every week. To this day, every time I smell roasting chicken, I think of sharing Shabbat dinner with my family." —Rabbi Ozur Bass

On a meat thermometer, the breast of a whole, fully cooked chicken should register 175°F (80°C).

"The best part about chicken soup for Shabbat is dunking the challah in it!" –Rabbi Ozur Bass

Always taste your soup as you cook so you can add salt or pepper as needed.

If you like your soup thicker, add more noodles.

chicken noodle soup

serves 6

Soup is delicious at Shabbat dinner. This recipe is quick to prepare because it uses already-cooked chicken. You can buy cooked chickens at the store or use leftovers.

get cooking...

1 Melt butter or margarine in a large saucepan over medium heat. Add onion and cook for 1 minute, then add celery and carrots. Cook vegetables until slightly translucent, about 4 more minutes.

2 Add cooked chicken, and stir in with vegetables for 2 minutes, so flavors mix together.

3 Add all broth and oregano, basil, bay leaves, and garlic powder.

4 Allow soup to simmer for 20 minutes at medium heat. Ten minutes prior to serving, adjust heat to medium-high and bring soup to a boil. Add uncooked noodles and cook for 10 minutes or according to package instructions.

ingredients...

1 tablespoon butter or margarine

½ cup chopped yellow onion

½ cup chopped celery

1 cup carrot, cut 1-inch (2.5-cm) thick

8 oz (225 g) cooked chicken meat, roughly pulled

3 14½-oz (430-ml) cans chicken broth

2 14½-oz (430-ml) cans vegetable broth

½ teaspoon dried oregano

½ teaspoon dried basil

2 bay leaves

¼ teaspoon garlic powder

6 oz (170 g) egg noodles, uncooked

Have a soup potluck party. Your friends can bring soups, salad, or bread, and you can serve them your chicken noodle soup.

This recipe is meat. For a Kosher meal, use margarine, vegetable oil, or olive oil.

matzoh balls

Matzoh balls are a delicious treat. The key to making fluffy, light matzoh balls is to pack them loosely. You want them to float when they cook. Matzoh balls almost double in size when they cook, so be sure not to make yours too big.

get cooking...

1 Separate 2 eggs and put the egg whites in a medium-sized mixing bowl. Set the yolks aside because you will add them later. Whisk the egg whites until they are light and fluffy.

2 Crack the last egg and combine with the yolks you set aside. Using a fork, beat together. Gently fold the yolks into your fluffy egg whites.

3 Add matzoh meal, vegetable oil, 2 tablespoons of chicken broth, water, salt, white pepper, and garlic powder, again folding it carefully into your mixture.

4 Place bowl in refrigerator for 1 hour, until the mixture is chilled and firm to the touch.

5 Place two quarts chicken broth in a large pot. Bring to a boil over medium-high heat.

6 Remove matzoh mixture from the refrigerator. Using your hands, scoop out a small bit of mixture and gently roll it in your hands to form a ball, about 1 inch (2.5 cm) in diameter. (Rinse your hands with cold water if the dough is sticking to your fingers.)

7 Using a slotted spoon, place matzoh balls into the chicken stock 1 at a time. Reduce heat so mixture is at a low simmer. Cover pot and allow matzoh balls to cook gently for about 45 minutes until they are cooked through.

8 Serve your matzoh balls in the broth they cooked in, or as a substitute for the noodles in chicken noodle soup.

ingredients...

3 eggs

1 cup matzoh meal

4 tablespoons vegetable oil

2 quarts plus 2 tablespoons chicken broth

½ cup cold water

1 teaspoon salt

½ teaspoon white pepper

½ teaspoon garlic powder

Knaidlach is the Yiddish word for "matzoh ball."

This recipe is meat. For a kosher meal, serve only with other meat or pareve foods.

Roll your matzoh balls gently.

"Most Jewish cooks have their own secrets as to how to make the best matzoh balls. One secret to light and fluffy balls is to substitute plain seltzer for the water." —Rabbi Ozur Bass

This recipe can be made vegetarian; just substitute vegetable broth for chicken broth.

This recipe is pareve and can be eaten with either meat or dairy meals.

If you use dried beans, soak and prepare them the night before.

vegetable cholent

Cholent is a great lunch for Shabbat because traditionally it cooks overnight, and is ready for the Saturday midday meal. Most cultures have similar long-cooking stew or bean dishes, such as French cassoulet or American baked beans. Cholent almost always features beans, barley, and hearty vegetables.

get cooking...

1 Heat vegetable oil in a large saucepan over medium-high heat. Add onion and cook until tender.

2 Add garlic, stirring often so it does not burn. Add mushrooms and continue to stir for 2 to 3 minutes or until mushrooms shrink down a bit. Reduce heat to medium.

3 Add beans, stirring gently. Add barley, carrots, and potatoes. Add salt and pepper, then vinegar, hot water, and broth. Be sure all vegetables are covered with liquid.

4 Turn heat to low and cover tightly. Traditionally, cholent is allowed to cook overnight. However, if left over medium heat, the cholent will be done in about 60 minutes.

ingredients...

⅓ cup vegetable oil

1 medium onion, cut into small chunks

2 cloves garlic, finely minced

1 cup baby portobella mushrooms, sliced

1 15-oz (425-g) can dark red kidney beans, rinsed

1 15-oz (425-g) can pinto beans, rinsed

½ cup whole barley, uncooked

4 carrots, cut into small chunks

5 medium potatoes, peeled and quartered

½ teaspoon salt, plus more if desired

1 teaspoon ground black pepper

⅓ cup red wine vinegar

1 cup very hot water

2 cups vegetable broth

"The word *cholent* is from the French meaning 'warm and slow cooking.' Because the pot is sealed and left to finish cooking overnight, it was one of the foods that was invented so Jewish people could follow the laws of Shabbat. Some villages had big ovens in the middle of the town where every family would bring their pots on Friday afternoon and leave them there until Saturday lunch."
—Rabbi Ozur Bass

shabbat ★

chickpea and couscous salad

This refreshing and colorful salad is perfect for *Seudah Shlishit* (pronounced *seh-oo-DAH shlee-SHEET*), a Shabbat meal eaten in the afternoon on Saturday. Eating three meals on Shabbat is considered a mitzvah, and *Seudah Shlishit* is the third meal.

This recipe is pareve and can be served with dairy or meat meals.

ingredients...

1 cup vegetable broth

1 cup uncooked instant couscous

3 tablespoons vegetable oil

2 tablespoons white vinegar

2 tablespoons lemon juice

1 teaspoon garlic powder

¼ cup fresh parsley, minced

¼ cup fresh basil, minced

1 15-oz (425-g) can chickpeas

4 plum tomatoes, diced

1 medium cucumber, diced

get cooking...

1 In a small saucepan, bring vegetable broth to a boil. While on the heat, stir in couscous. Immediately cover pot, turn off stove, and remove saucepan from heat so liquid is absorbed into couscous. When all liquid is absorbed, fluff up couscous using a fork. Be careful because the saucepan is hot. Set couscous aside and allow it to cool.

2 Combine oil, vinegar, lemon juice, and garlic powder in a mixing bowl. Gently fold in the parsley and basil.

3 Add chickpeas, tomatoes, and cucumber to the cooled couscous. Mix in oil and vinegar mixture.

4 Cover with plastic wrap and refrigerate. Serve cold.

Chickpeas can be found in traditional recipes around the world. They're also known as garbanzo beans and ceci beans.

"We will often invite over our neighbors and have a potluck meal of leftover Shabbat dinner and Saturday lunch for our *Seudah Shlishit.*" —Rabbi Ozur Bass

If you do not have vegetable broth, you can use water to make the couscous instead.

ROSH HASHANAH

L'Shanah tovah! Happy New Year! Rosh Hashanah brings families together to celebrate the autumn harvest and a sweet new year with brisket, tzimmes, sweet potato casserole, honey cake, and more!

Rosh Hashanah is the Jewish New Year. It celebrates the anniversary of God creating the world, and looks ahead to making the new year better. This is a time of celebration and reflection.

Along with any good celebration comes good food! Naturally sweet foods like honey, apples, raisins, and carrots are served at Rosh Hashanah, to remind us of the sweet things that lie ahead. Often, Rosh Hashanah feasts begin by dipping apples in honey, and saying a prayer asking God for a wonderful year.

There are many food traditions followed during Rosh Hashanah.

Families cook together for the new year meal.

> "Having a big celebratory dinner with friends and family is the best way to remember why it is important to keep our relationships healthy."
> –Rabbi Ozur Bass

For instance, challot are often baked in a circular shape, which symbolizes the crown of God. When eaten during the new year celebration, challah is dipped in honey.

Pomegranates and their many seeds (called "arils") are symbols of blessings in the new year. These Mediterranean fruits are in season starting in October, and so dishes containing pomegranate seeds are often eaten at Rosh Hashanah.

Some Jewish communities have the custom of eating different foods and blessing one another with ideas about the food itself. For example, they will eat from the head of a fish and say, "May it be your will that we be like the head (leaders) and not the tail (followers)." Other families eat the head of a fish—or simply place one on the table—to represent the "head" or beginning of the year.

What Rosh Hashanah traditions does your family celebrate?

sweet ginger gefilte fish

Gefilte fish is made from finely chopped fish that has been cooked with onions and carrots. Sweetened by orange juice and honey, this gefilte fish recipe can help you welcome a sweet new year.

ingredients...

1 16-oz (450-g) loaf gefilte fish, defrosted

1 tablespoon fresh ginger, grated

¼ cup soy sauce

¼ cup orange juice

¼ cup honey

1 tablespoon brown sugar

get cooking...

1 Preheat oven to 350°F (180°C).

2 Press fish into a jelly roll pan or round cake pan.

3 Whisk remaining ingredients in bowl and pour on top of fish.

4 Cover with foil and bake for 30 to 35 minutes, until heated through.

5 For a twist, you can cut your finished gefilte fish into fun shapes with cookie cutters!

Be gentle with your gefilte shapes!

Frozen gefilte fish loaves can be found in kosher grocery stores or the kosher section of some large grocery stores. If you can't find them, jarred gefilte fish will work just fine.

" Gefilte fish is one of the many foods whose recipe shows where a family came from in eastern Europe. Jews from Poland eat their gefilte fish sweet, whereas Lithuanian and Russian Jews eat it with no sugar and more pepper." —Rabbi Ozur Bass

rosh hashanah

This recipe is pareve and can be served with either dairy or meat meals.

Most gefilte fish is made of carp and whitefish.

soda pop brisket

This is a traditional Jewish dish and a real crowd pleaser. Your friends and family will be surprised to learn that the secret ingredient is cola!

ingredients...

1 medium onion, sliced into rings

3- to 4-pound (1.3- to 1.8-kg) flat
   brisket, trimmed

2 cloves of garlic, minced

2 tablespoons yellow mustard

1 tablespoon Worcestershire sauce

1 tablespoon olive oil

1 cup soda, cola flavored (not diet)

parsley for garnish (optional)

get cooking...

1 Preheat oven to 350°F (180°C).

2 Line baking sheet with aluminum foil. Place half of onion slices on baking sheet, and place brisket, fat side up, on top of onions.

3 In small bowl or measuring cup, stir together garlic, mustard, Worcestershire sauce, olive oil, and soda.

4 Pour mixture over top of brisket and place remaining onion slices on top. Cover with foil.

Pour slowly!

Let meat sit for about 10 minutes before you cut it.

Cover the whole brisket.

5 Bake for 2 hours, or until the meat reaches an internal temperature of 175°F (80°C).

To serve brisket, slice it thinly across the grain.

"The word *tzimmes* is one of those great Yiddish words that has come to mean many different things. It can be used to mean trouble, or a whole lot of something, or a big deal, as in 'Don't make such a big tzimmes over all of this!'"   –Rabbi Ozur Bass

Some people cook a piece of beef in tzimmes to impart a meaty flavor.

sweet carrot tzimmes

Tzimmes (pronounced *SIM-iss*) sounds like how it is prepared: simmered! The longer you cook it, the more like a thick sauce it will become. You can serve it chunky, like ours, or blend it smooth. Every family has their own special way of preparing tzimmes.

get cooking...

1 Combine all ingredients in a saucepan, making sure that the carrots and fruit are covered in liquid.

2 Bring to a boil. Allow mixture to boil for 10 minutes.

3 Reduce heat and allow mixture to simmer, uncovered, for 25 to 35 minutes or until the liquid evaporates and the tzimmes thickens.

ingredients...

1½ pounds (680 g) carrots, sliced into coins

½ cup dried cranberries

½ cup dried apricots, diced

¼ cup golden raisins

¼ cup raisins

½ teaspoon salt

½ teaspoon cinnamon

1 11-oz (325-ml) can apricot nectar

1 cup water

This recipe is pareve, and may be served with meat or dairy foods.

Although it is served at almost every holiday, tzimmes is very common at Rosh Hashanah because it helps everyone start the new year on a sweet note. It is also served at Passover because it is a great topping for matzoh!

rosh hashanah ✷

37

harvest rice with pomegranate seeds

The beautiful seeds of a pomegranate are called "arils." They look like shiny red jewels in this holiday rice that celebrates the rich harvest at the beginning of a new year.

ingredients...

2 tablespoons olive oil

½ cup onion, chopped

½ cup celery, chopped

1 cup apple, chopped

¼ cup dried cherries

¼ cup pecans, chopped

1 6- to 8-oz (170- to 225-g) package quick-cook rice pilaf mix, regular or vegetable flavor

½ cup pomegranate arils

get cooking...

1 Heat oil in a medium-sized sauté pan over medium-high heat.

2 Add onion, celery, and apple, and cook until soft and translucent, stirring frequently. Reduce heat to medium, and add cherries and pecans.

3 Set mixture aside on plate.

4 Using the same pan, prepare rice according to package directions.

5 To remove arils, have an adult cut the crown off of a pomegranate, and break the fruit into segments. Holding segments over a bowl, use fingers or a spoon to scoop out seeds.

The arils are easy to scoop out.

6 Add arils and the fruit-and-vegetable mixture to cooked rice, stirring to combine.

For a kosher meal, serve with either meat or dairy foods, as this recipe is pareve.

If you can't find fresh pomegranates, you can use frozen arils, which are available year-round

"Pomegranates, with their many seeds, are a traditional Rosh Hashanah fruit. They represent wishes for a year filled with many wonderful new beginnings. In Hebrew the word for *pomegranate* is 'Rimon,' which means 'crown.' We eat the *Rimon* to crown the head of the Jewish year." —Rabbi Ozur Bass

sweet potato casserole

With a crisp, candylike topping, this vegetable dish is an extra sweet way to welcome the new year. You can use baked, boiled, or canned sweet potatoes.

ingredients...

3 cups cooked sweet potatoes, mashed
½ cup brown sugar
½ cup butter, melted
½ cup milk
2 eggs
1 teaspoon vanilla extract

For the topping:
¾ cup brown sugar
⅓ cup all-purpose flour
⅓ cup butter, melted
1 cup pecans, roughly chopped

get cooking...

1 Preheat oven to 350°F (180°C).

2 In mixing bowl, combine mashed sweet potatoes with brown sugar, melted butter, milk, eggs, and vanilla. Break up any chunks of sweet potato with your spoon. Mixture should be totally smooth.

3 In a separate bowl, use fingers to combine brown sugar, flour, melted butter, and pecans for the topping. Set aside.

4 Spoon sweet potato mixture into oven-safe dish, and sprinkle pecan mixture evenly on top.

5 Bake for 30 to 35 minutes, until sweet potatoes are warmed through and the topping has formed a crust.

"My family loves to serve this with marshmallows instead of pecans. After preparing the sweet potatoes and warming them through, top with marshmallows and put under the broiler just long enough for the marshmallows to brown."
-Rabbi Ozur Bass

To prepare mashed sweet potatoes, scrub potatoes well and microwave for 6 to 8 minutes or until potatoes are soft throughout. Sweet potatoes can also be boiled for 20 to 24 minutes or until soft. Canned sweet potatoes work beautifully, as well.

This recipe is dairy. For a kosher meal, serve only with other dairy or pareve foods.

Sprinkle on a little cayenne for a spicy twist!

Top your honey lemon cake with a light sprinkling of powdered sugar.

honey lemon cake

"Every Jewish cook I know has a different version of honey cake. It wouldn't be Rosh Hashanah without this dessert! I like to have a slice of honey cake with cream cheese on it for breakfast before going to services for Rosh Hashanah."
-Rabbi Ozur Bass

Don't wait for Rosh Hashanah to make this delicious cake. You can bake this moist, spicy dessert any time.

get cooking...

1   Preheat oven to 350°F (180°C). Oil and flour a 9 x 13–inch (23 x 33–cm) baking pan or a bundt pan (as shown).

2   Combine sugar, honey, vegetable oil, eggs, lemon zest, and juice. Stir well.

3   In another bowl, combine flour, baking powder, baking soda, salt, and cinnamon. Add this mixture slowly to honey mixture, combining well. Stir in the water.

4   Pour into prepared baking pan and bake for 35 to 40 minutes.

ingredients...

½ cup sugar

1 cup honey

½ cup vegetable oil

3 eggs

2 teaspoons grated lemon zest

¼ cup lemon juice

3 cups all-purpose flour

3 teaspoons baking powder

1 teaspoon baking soda

½ teaspoon salt

1 teaspoon cinnamon

¼ cup water

To test a cake for doneness, insert a wooden toothpick into center of cake. It should come out clean when done.

Get all of that batter in there!

This recipe is pareve and may be served with either dairy or meat meals.

YOM KIPPUR

Families fast during Yom Kippur, and attend services at synagogue. When the fast is over, everyone comes together for delicious bagels, egg dishes, kugel, and more.

Second to Shabbat, Yom Kippur is the holiest day of the Jewish year. During the ten days before Yom Kippur, Jewish people think about their behavior over the past year. They apologize to other people for anything they have done wrong. On Yom Kippur itself, they apologize to God and try to figure out how to to avoid the same mistakes over the next year.

During Yom Kippur, people fast, which means they do not eat or drink anything from sunset until sunset the next day. The fast is a way to focus people's minds on who they would like to become rather than simpler things like what they're going to eat. Of course hungry fasters often think about *when* they'll eat again! In fact, some synagogues pass around small boxes that contain cinnamon and cloves. These are called *B'samim* boxes. People sniff the spices, which helps ease their hunger during services.

The long day of prayer and fasting ends when the shofar—a ram's horn—is blown. At the sound of the shofar, everyone's serious mood is broken and there is a sense of joy that comes over the community. People get together at one another's homes to break their day-long fast. Some synagogues have potluck break-the-fast meals so that the whole community

"Some people say *Tzom Kal,* or 'have an easy fast' at Yom Kippur. I like to say 'Have a meaningful fast.'" –Rabbi Ozur Bass

can share this time together.

Because Yom Kippur is a holy day and no food can be cooked, food is prepared before the holiday begins. Eating lighter foods like eggs, kugel, and pastries is traditional (and is easier on an empty stomach than heavy foods). Breaking the fast is a welcome celebration at the end of a serious holiday.

Light foods, such as bagels and cream cheese, are often eaten to break the fast.

bagels with cream cheese

Turn your kitchen into a bagel shop by making hot, fresh, chewy bagels, complete with your own homemade flavored cream cheeses!

get cooking...

1 Pour warm water into large mixing bowl, then add yeast and stir until dissolved.

2 Add malt, flour, and salt, and mix until dough forms. Knead for 10 minutes, until dough is no longer sticky.

3 Use fingers to oil the inside of the bowl lightly. Place dough back in bowl and set aside for 1 hour to rise.

4 Divide risen dough into 8 equal pieces and form into balls. Cover with plastic wrap and set aside for 30 minutes.

5 To boil the bagels, add water, malt, and brown sugar to a large saucepan. Bring to a boil.

6 Preheat oven to 450°F (230°C). Line two baking sheets with parchment paper.

7 Uncover dough balls. Poke a hole about 2 inches (5 cm) in diameter in middle of dough ball to form bagel. Have an adult place them in the boiling water and cook for 1 minute on each side.

8 Remove bagels from water with slotted spoon and place on baking sheet. Leave room between bagels. Bake for 15 minutes or until bagels are a deep golden color, then turn over and bake for 5 to 7 more minutes until other side is golden.

ingredients...

1½ cups warm water

1 tablespoon instant yeast

1 tablespoon malted milk powder

4½ cups bread flour

2 teaspoons salt

2 teaspoons vegetable oil

For boiling bagels:

2 quarts water

1 tablespoon malted milk powder

1 tablespoon brown sugar

Flavored Cream Cheeses

To make your very own flavored cream cheese spreads, simply add the following ingredients to 4 oz (112 g) of softened cream cheese:

Honey Nut Spread
2 tablespoons walnuts, finely chopped
1 tablespoon honey
1 tablespoon brown sugar

Strawberry Spread
¼ cup strawberries, finely chopped
1 tablespoon confectioner's sugar

Garden Vegetable Spread
3 tablespoons carrot, finely minced
2 tablespoons broccoli, finely chopped
1 tablespoon red onion, finely minced

Cinnamon Raisin Spread
3 tablespoons raisins, finely chopped
1 tablespoon brown sugar
½ teaspoon cinnamon

Homemade bagels are the best!

To add poppy or sesame seeds, carefully press one side of bagel into a dish of seeds just before baking.

This recipe is pareve, and may be served with either dairy or meat.

smoked salmon frittata

This creamy egg dish tastes like an omelet and is easy to make. Make two or three to serve all your break-the-fast party guests.

ingredients...

6 eggs, beaten

½ cup sour cream

1 teaspoon dried dill

2 tablespoons butter

½ cup smoked salmon, chopped

¼ cup onion, finely chopped

¼ cup cream cheese, cut
into small pieces

get cooking...

1 Preheat oven broiler.

2 Whisk together eggs, sour cream, and dill in bowl.

3 Melt butter in 12-inch (30-cm) oven-safe sauté pan over medium heat. Add salmon and onion, and cook for 2 to 3 minutes.

4 Pour egg mixture into pan and drop pieces of cream cheese into eggs. Cook for about 5 minutes or until eggs become firm.

5 Place pan under broiler for 3 to 4 minutes, until frittata is lightly browned and puffed.

This recipe is dairy. For a kosher meal, serve only with other dairy or pareve foods.

This recipe can be made a day in advance and stored in the refrigerator. Reheat before serving by placing under broiler for about 2 minutes, or until warmed through.

"Many people serve bagels with cream cheese and lox at a break fast. This recipe is a clever way to combine all those tastes together in one dish!"   –Rabbi Ozur Bass

Be sure to use a pot holder when removing pan from oven. The handle will be very very hot!

"Kugel is one of the most popular and well-known Jewish foods. When it has dried fruit in it, it is called *Yerushalmi*, which means 'from Jerusalem.'" –Rabbi Ozur Bass

This recipe is dairy. For a kosher meal, serve only with other dairy or pareve foods.

Al dente means "to the tooth," which means to cook the pasta until firm.

basic any-which-way kugel

Kugel is a baked egg-and-noodle dish that can be sweet or savory. Everyone has his or her favorite ingredients. With this recipe, you can make one delicious kugel or custom-make mini kugels to suit everyone's tastes!

get cooking...

1 Preheat the oven to 350°F (180°C). Lightly grease a 9-inch (23-cm) square pan.

2 Bring a saucepan of water to a boil. Cook the noodles according to package instructions until they are al dente, then drain.

3 In a large bowl, stir together butter, cream cheese, sour cream, eggs, sugar, vanilla, and cinnamon. Add apple cider and milk, stirring to combine. Gently stir in noodles.

4 If you're adding mix-ins, do that now (see sidebar).

5 Transfer noodle mixture to baking pan.

6 In a small bowl, combine cornflake crumbs, butter, sugar, brown sugar, vanilla, and cinnamon. Spread topping over noodle mixture.

7 Bake for about 50 minutes or until kugel is bubbly and golden.

8 Let cool for 10 minutes.

ingredients...

For noodle mixture:

1 8-oz (225-g) package of broad egg noodles

½ cup butter, softened

1 8-oz (225-g) package of cream cheese, softened

1 cup sour cream

4 eggs, slightly beaten

½ cup sugar

1½ teaspoons vanilla extract

1 teaspoon cinnamon

1 cup apple cider

½ cup milk

For basic topping:

1½ cups cornflake crumbs

½ cup butter, softened

¼ cup sugar

¼ cup brown sugar

1 teaspoon vanilla extract

1 teaspoon cinnamon

Make customized mini kugels!

Use the same measurements as the regular recipe, except reduce your liquids to:

¼ cup apple cider

3 tablespoons milk

Lightly grease small oven-proof dishes or disposable foil mini pie pans.

Follow steps 1 through 3. Then:

4. Add 1 tablespoon of mix-ins, such as crushed pineapple, maraschino cherries, mini chocolate chips, preserves or jam, maple syrup, shredded apple, raisins, dried fruit, almond slivers, or pecans.

5. Top with cornflake-crumb mixture or more of your mix-ins.

6. Place containers on a baking sheet and put in the oven. Bake for about 12 minutes or until kugels are bubbly and golden.

mandel bread

Sometimes called mondel bread or *Mandelbrot*, this cookie is very much like Italian biscotti. It is baked twice to make it very crunchy.

ingredients...

3 eggs

¾ cup sugar

2 teaspoons vanilla

¾ cup vegetable oil

3½ cups all-purpose flour

2 teaspoons baking powder

¼ teaspoon cinnamon

½ cup almond slivers

For the topping:

¼ cup sugar

2 teaspoons cinnamon

"Be sure to make enough mandel bread so that there is some left for breakfast the next day. It's great warm from the toaster with butter on top."
—Rabbi Ozur Bass

get cooking...

1 Preheat oven to 350°F (180°C).

2 Beat eggs and sugar in medium mixing bowl until light and fluffy. Add vanilla and oil. Sift flour, baking powder, and cinnamon into wet mixture. Stir until combined. Gently stir in almonds.

3 Separate dough into two equal portions. Shape each portion into a rectangle about 5 inches x 10 inches (12.5 cm x 25 cm), and 1-inch (2.5-cm) thick. Place them on an ungreased baking sheet.

4 Combine remaining sugar and cinnamon in a small bowl. Sprinkle over dough rectangles. You can top with almond slivers, if you like.

5 Measuring with a ruler, mark the dough at 1-inch (2.5-cm) intervals. This will create guides for cutting the cookies after baking.

An adult can mark the dough with a knife.

6 Bake for 20 minutes until golden and firm to the touch. Remove from oven. Using a large spatula, move cookie rectangles to cutting board. An adult should carefully slice through the marks, creating long, 1-inch (2.5-cm)–wide cookies. Then place cookies, cut side down, back on warm baking sheet and return to oven.

7 Bake cookies again until they are golden and toasted, up to 10 minutes.

Mandel means "almond" in German.

yom kippur

52

You can substitute ½ cup of chocolate chips for almonds, if you like.

SUKKOT

Bundled up in their sukkah, Jewish families celebrate the abundance of autumn foods. Sukkot brings hearty pumpkin soup, stuffed cabbage, stuffed apples, and happy, stuffed bellies!

Sukkot celebrates the fall harvest and connects us to the Earth. One of the symbols during this holiday is the symbol of the four species, called the

Baked apples are a favorite Sukkot treat!

lulav and *etrog.* The *lulav* is made of three plants—palm, willow, and myrtle branches. An *etrog* is a fruit that looks and smells like a large lemon. When Jewish people wave these four species, they are asking God to help provide enough rain so that the crops can grow and there will be enough food for the year.

The Hebrew word *sukkot* means "many booths." The Jewish tradition teaches that a sukkah is a booth or tent in which our Israelite ancestors lived as they wandered in the desert after leaving Egypt. During Sukkot, families build similar booths in their

"We try to replace our home with our sukkah during Sukkot. We bring out our best dishes and have elaborate meals in our sukkah. And as long as the weather is good, we spend the night in the sukkah, too!" —Rabbi Ozur Bass

yards, and decorate them with drawings, paper chains, strings of popcorn, and fruits and vegetables.

There are many traditions that are followed during Sukkot. For instance, the roof of a sukkah must be made of plants that have been cut down. And there must be just the right amount of coverage: You want shade to protect from the sun, but you also want to make sure that a person sitting in the sukkah can see the stars at night. The best part of having a sukkah is relaxing in it and visiting with friends.

Eating in your sukkah is fun, too. Meals usually include seasonal fruits and vegetables, and should be easy to eat outside. Foods like *holishkes* (cabbage rolls) are especially festive, because they are like little cornucopias, stuffed with plenty.

Pomegranates are a symbol of plenty.

pumpkin soup

Pumpkin soup is a terrific dish to enjoy in your sukkah, and it will keep you warm on a chilly day. Add a spinach salad filled with fruits and nuts to make it a meal. Enjoy an assortment of quick breads like cranberry, cinnamon raisin, and banana nut with your soup.

ingredients...

3 tablespoons butter

1 medium onion, finely chopped

1 clove garlic, finely chopped

1 tablespoon brown sugar

1 cup potato, peeled and shredded

1 cup apple, peeled and shredded

1 14½-oz (430-ml) can vegetable broth

½ cup water

½ teaspoon salt

¼ teaspoon ground black pepper

1 15-oz (425-g) can cooked canned unsweetened pumpkin (not pie filling)

1 12-oz (350-ml) can evaporated milk

⅛ teaspoon ground cinnamon

⅛ teaspoon ground nutmeg

get cooking...

1 Melt butter in large saucepan over medium heat.

2 Add onion, garlic, and brown sugar to saucepan and cook until soft, about 4 minutes.

3 Add potato and apple, and cook until tender, about 1 to 2 minutes.

4 Add broth, water, salt, and pepper.

5 Turn heat to medium-high and bring mixture to a boil, stirring occasionally.

6 Reduce heat and cook for 15 minutes on low, stirring occasionally.

7 Stir in pumpkin, evaporated milk, cinnamon, and nutmeg.

8 After a few minutes, taste soup. If soup is too thick, add ¼ cup water. If it's too thin, add a ¼ cup more evaporated milk. Cook for 5 more minutes on low.

This recipe is dairy. For a kosher meal, serve only with other dairy or pareve foods.

"A good hearty soup is definitely a plus on a cold fall night. It's fun to invite people over and form a line to pass along the food from the kitchen to the sukkah."

-Rabbi Ozur Bass

Chicken broth can be used in place of vegetable broth; however, the soup would not be kosher.

Cabbage rolls can be made in advance and refrigerated for a day before they are baked.

holishkes (cabbage rolls)

This cabbage roll, or stuffed cabbage, is like a miniature meatloaf wrapped in a cabbage leaf. It's extra delicious when drenched in a tangy sweet-and-sour sauce.

serves
6

get cooking...

1 Preheat oven to 350°F (180°C).

2 Combine rice, egg, water, onion, garlic, and beef in mixing bowl.

3 Separate the mixture into 12 portions. Scoop each portion into middle of a wilted cabbage leaf, roll, and tuck ends under. Line up the rolls in your pan, seam side down.

4 Combine crushed tomatoes, tomato sauce, lemon juice, brown sugar, and Worcestershire sauce in small bowl. Pour mixture over cabbage rolls.

5 Cover dish with foil and bake for 60 minutes.

ingredients...

1 cup cooked rice

1 egg, beaten

½ cup water

½ cup onion, minced

1 clove garlic, minced

1 pound (450 g) ground beef

12 cabbage leaves, wilted

For the sauce:

1 28-oz (800-g) can crushed tomatoes

1 8-oz (225-g) can tomato sauce

2 tablespoons lemon juice

2 tablespoons brown sugar

1 tablespoon Worcestershire sauce

"Stuffed cabbage always reminds me of sleeping in a sleeping bag. It's a perfect symbolic meal to eat when we spend the night in our sleeping bags in the sukkah!"
—Rabbi Ozur Bass

To wilt cabbage leaves, place a whole head of cabbage in the freezer the night before you make the recipe. Remove the cabbage 3 hours before you need it. The leaves will peel off easily.

For a kosher meal, serve only with other meat or pareve foods.

baked stuffed apples

Sukkot is all about enjoying the bounty of autumn. What better way to celebrate than to go apple picking with your friends and family, and then make a delicious dessert out of your very own harvest?

ingredients...

6 apples, cored

½ cup quick-cook oats

¾ cup brown sugar

2 tablespoons lemon juice

1 tablespoon maple syrup

2 teaspoons cinnamon

6 tablespoons butter

1 pint vanilla ice cream (optional)

get cooking...

1 Preheat oven to 400°F (200°C). Place cored apples in baking dish.

2 In a small bowl, combine oats, brown sugar, lemon juice, maple syrup, cinnamon, and butter. Pack mixture into apples.

3 Bake for 18 to 22 minutes or until apples are soft.

4 Place apples in individual bowls and top each with a scoop of ice cream.

When baking with apples, select apples with firm flesh, such as Rome Beauty, Cortland, and Granny Smith.

Be careful! Apples and filling are hot!

This recipe is dairy. For a kosher meal, use margarine instead of butter and leave out the ice cream, or serve only with dairy or pareve foods.

HANUKKAH

Families gather around the warm glow of menorah candles during this winter holiday. Delicious fried latkes, doughnuts, and savory dumplings warm everyone's belly, while spending time with family and giving gifts warm everyone's heart!

Hanukkah, or the Festival of Lights, is an eight-day celebration that reminds us of the importance of faith and hope.

In ancient times, a Syrian ruler named Antiochus controlled Israel and did not want anyone to practice Judaism. However, a Jewish leader named Mattathias and his sons, including Judah Maccabee, led a successful revolt against Antiochus. Throughout his life, Judah Maccabee and his brothers continued to fight against Antiochus, eventually winning power and taking back the Temple in Jerusalem. The holiday of Hanukkah recalls the miracle of this military victory against impossible odds. It also celebrates the idea of lighting the lights of God even in the darkest of nights. We remember this by lighting the menorah for the eight nights of Hanukkah.

Jewish tradition teaches that when the Temple was recaptured and was to be rededicated to the Jews of Israel, only one day's worth of oil was found to light the lamps.

Miraculously, the oil lasted eight days.

"There is a wonderful tradition in honor of the heroism of Judith: women should not do any work while the menorah lights are burning."
– Rabbi Ozur Bass

Because oil is an important part of the Hanukkah story, food cooked in oil is part of Hanukkah celebrations. Latkes, doughnuts, and Israeli *sufganiyot* are all cooked in oil.

Besides food, there are other wonderful Hanukkah traditions. Each night of the holiday, Jews around the world light another one of the eight candles on the menorah. The menorah is often kept in a window so that the miracles of Hanukkah are announced to the world.

While the latkes are frying and the menorah is lighting the night, families love to play dreidel, which is a game of

Fried *ponchik* are a sweet treat!

chance. The reward is a stack of chocolate coins called gelt (and bragging rights, of course).

While many people love sweet applesauce with their latkes, some prefer savory sour cream with chives. Why not try both?

potato latkes with applesauce

Potato pancakes, or latkes, are perhaps the most recognizable Jewish food. Carrying on the Hanukkah tradition of frying foods in oil, latkes are crispy and delicious.

potato latkes:

1 Shred potatoes with a grater. Watch your fingers!

2 Put potatoes and onion on paper towels and squeeze out the liquid.

3 Put dried potatoes and onion in medium bowl, then add egg, flour, and salt. Combine well.

4 Heat half of canola oil in skillet until very hot, then scoop mounds of potato mixture (about 2 tablespoons each) into pan. Do not crowd pan.

5 Press mounds down with spatula to flatten. Reduce heat and cook until bottoms are golden, about 5 minutes. Flip latkes and cook until golden on other side, then remove cooked latkes to a paper towel to drain. Repeat, using remaining canola oil as needed.

6 Serve immediately, or transfer to an oven-safe dish and keep in a warm (250°F or 120°C) oven until ready to serve.

applesauce:

1 Stir together all ingredients in a medium saucepan.

2 Cover saucepan and cook over medium heat for 15 to 20 minutes, or until apples are soft. (This will depend on the type of apples you use.) Remove from heat and allow mixture to cool.

3 Using a potato masher, mash mixture until your applesauce is as chunky or smooth as you like.

"As the latkes are frying, everyone gathers in the kitchen and tells stories, plays dreidel, and gives presents to celebrate the joy of bringing the light of the menorah into a dark time of year."
-Rabbi Ozur Bass

ingredients...

For the latkes:

1 pound (450 g) potatoes, peeled

½ cup onion, finely chopped

1 large egg, beaten

2 tablespoons all-purpose flour

½ teaspoon salt

½ cup canola oil

For the applesauce:

4 apples, peeled, cored, and diced

¾ cup water

1 tablespoon brown sugar

½ teaspoon ground cinnamon

This recipe is pareve, and may be served with meat or dairy meals.

hanukkah

savory cheese sufganiyot

An unusual twist on the classic Israeli *sufganiyot* (pronounced *SUF-gan-yot*), our version of this recipe has a cheese filling that recalls the story of Judith's bravery as she fed rich cheeses to Holofernes.

serves 5

get cooking...

1 In a small bowl, mix together softened cream cheese, cheddar cheese, and parsley.

2 Separate biscuits and flatten each one so diameter is about 4 inches (10 cm). Place about a tablespoon of the cheese mixture on a biscuit. Place another biscuit on top and pinch edges together so cheese is fully enclosed. Repeat until you have 5 *sufganiyot*.

3 Heat the oil in a saucepan to 350°F (180°C). While waiting for oil to heat, line a baking sheet with paper towels.

4 When oil is ready, have an adult use a slotted spoon to lower *sufganiyot* into oil. Cook for 2 to 3 minutes on each side, until the dough is cooked through and golden brown on both sides.

5 Remove *sufganiyot* from oil with slotted spoon and place on baking sheet. While still hot, sprinkle with salt.

ingredients...

3 oz (85 g) cream cheese, softened

1 cup mild cheddar cheese, grated

1 teaspoon dried parsley

1 (10 count) package of pre-made refrigerated biscuits

24 oz (710 ml) canola oil (for frying)

2 teaspoons salt

Note: you can find pre-made biscuits in the refrigerated section of most supermarkets.

This recipe is dairy. For a kosher meal, serve only with other dairy or pareve foods.

Sufganiyot are traditionally stuffed with jelly. This is a savory version.

"Hanukkah in Israel is usually cold and rainy. There is nothing better to warm your insides than getting fresh, steaming-hot *sufganiyot!*"
—Rabbi Ozur Bass

raspberry ponchik

Polish *ponchik* are fried doughnuts stuffed with jelly. Eastern European Jews brought these with them as they moved to Israel. This quick and easy recipe allows anyone to celebrate Hanukkah with homemade jelly doughnuts.

get cooking...

1 Separate biscuits and flatten them so diameter is about 4 inches (10 cm).

2 Place about a teaspoon of jelly or jam in the center of each biscuit. Bring the edges together to form a ball. Pinch it closed at the top to seal in the filling.

Don't overload the *ponchik*.

3 When all 10 *ponchik* are ready, pour the oil in a saucepan and bring to 350°F (180°C). While waiting for oil to reach temperature, pour sugar and cinnamon onto a plate.

4 When oil is ready, have an adult use a slotted spoon to lower *ponchik* into oil. Cook for about 2 minutes on each side, until the dough is cooked through and golden brown.

5 Remove from oil with slotted spoon and place on plate with cinnamon sugar. Gently roll the *ponchik* to coat. Be careful, *ponchik* will be hot!

ingredients...

1 (10 count) package of pre-made refrigerated biscuits

24 oz (710 ml) canola oil (for frying)

¼ cup raspberry jelly or jam

¼ cup sugar

2 teaspoons cinnamon

Note: you can use any flavor of your favorite jelly, jam, or preserve.

This recipe is dairy. To plan a kosher meal, serve only with other dairy or pareve foods.

Ponchik are the eastern European version of Israeli *sufganiyot*.

"A great trick to remove some of the oil from the cooked *ponchik* is to put the cinnamon and sugar in a paper bag. When the *ponchik* are done, toss them in the bag and gently shake. The *ponchik* will get coated in cinnamon sugar, and the bag will absorb some of the oil."
—Rabbi Ozur Bass

TU B'SHEVAT

Wheat, barley, figs, and dates play a leading role in Tu B'Shevat meals. If the weather's nice enough, plan a picnic to celebrate the trees in your yard or favorite park. If it's still too cold, have an indoor picnic, complete with blanket, basket, and friends!

Tu B'Shevat is a unique festival that celebrates the birthdays of trees. It occurs at the beginning of spring in Israel, just as trees begin to bloom, and is celebrated by enjoying the outdoors and planting trees. In other parts of the world, however, Tu B'Shevat takes place while it is still too cold to plant trees. Still, the holiday reminds us to remember the land of Israel and that spring is on its way.

If it's too cold to plant a tree where you live, you can celebrate Tu B'Shevat by planting herb seeds in a paper cup and sitting them on a windowsill to grow. If you plant parsley, you can use

Cooking with friends makes every meal special.

"In Hebrew school when I was growing up, our teachers always gave us *bukser* to eat. I never really wanted to try it. Only when I got older did I learn that *bukser* was a dried carob pod. I love to crunch on them now!" —Rabbi Ozur Bass

your harvest a few months later at your Pesach seder.

If planting isn't your thing, another way to celebrate is by giving a plant to someone you love.

Eating fresh fruits is also an important part of this holiday. Some people plan a special meal—like a Pesach seder—that features wheat, barley, grapes, figs, pomegranates, olives, and dates. These foods are called the "seven species," and are important crops in Israel. Tu B'Shevat is our way to celebrate them. Rabbis teach that even when we aren't in Israel, just the act of eating any of these foods is a way to remember and praise the land of Israel.

Another food that is in season during Tu B'Shevat is carob. It grows in a pod and tastes a bit like chocolate. Carob pods are sometimes dried themselves, and then eaten as well. Dried carob pods are called *bukser*, and are sort of dry and very crunchy.

No matter the fresh fruits or grains that you cook with for Tu B'Shevat, honoring nature and one another is the real spirit of this holiday.

fig spread and tu b'shevat granola

Figs and walnuts taste delicious with cream cheese. Together with granola they make an excellent snack to enjoy while sitting under a tree during Tu B'Shevat. Try the spread on baguette and apple slices.

ingredients...

For the granola:

4 cups oatmeal (not quick oats)

½ cup canola oil

¾ cup brown sugar

2 tablespoons honey

2 tablespoons maple syrup

1½ teaspoons cinnamon

1 teaspoon vanilla extract

½ cup raisins (optional)

¼ cup almonds, slivered (optional)

For the fig spread:

1 cup dried figs, stems removed

⅓ cup walnuts

8 oz (225 g) cream cheese

¼ teaspoon salt

tu b'shevat granola:

1 Preheat oven to 350°F (180°C).

2 Combine oatmeal, canola oil, brown sugar, honey, maple syrup, cinnamon, and vanilla in bowl. Break up any clumps of brown sugar.

3 Pour mixture onto baking sheet. Bake in oven for about 20 minutes, stirring every 5 minutes. Be careful not to burn it.

4 After the mixture is baked, add raisins and almonds (if using). Then pour onto wax paper to cool. Serve warm or at room temperature.

fig spread:

1 Chop figs in food processor until fine. Add walnuts and pulse until walnuts are coarsely chopped. Add cream cheese and salt and process until combined.

2 Put mixture in small bowl. Cover with plastic wrap and chill in refrigerator for 1 hour before serving.

Fig spread is dairy and may be served with other dairy or pareve dishes.

"After the granola mixture bakes, you can add anything you want. Dried cherries, puffed rice cereal, toasted coconut, or chocolate chips are all delicious options."
—Rabbi Ozur Bass

Granola is pareve and may be eaten with dairy or meat dishes.

Granola tastes great sprinkled on yogurt.

You can use 3 fresh figs in place of dried figs.

Decorate the cake with frosting or candy leaves, or use real hazelnuts.

hazelnut tree birthday cake

serves **10**

At Tu B'Shevat we learn about the symbolism of hazelnuts. They have edible insides that represent holiness, and outer shells that serves as protection. Since Tu B'Shevat celebrates the birthdays of trees, a birthday cake makes the day even more fun.

get cooking...

1 Preheat oven to 350°F (180°C). Line jelly roll pan with parchment paper.

2 Combine cake mix, eggs, water, and oil and beat until smooth. Pour batter into pan.

3 Bake for about 15 minutes or until done. Let cool for 5 minutes.

4 Turn cake out onto a dish towel. Peel off baked-on parchment paper.

5 While still warm, carefully roll towel and cake lengthwise. Set aside. Allow rolled cake to cool for 30 minutes.

Let the towel help you roll the cake.

6 In another bowl, combine frosting and hazelnut-flavored spread using wooden spoon.

7 Unroll cooled cake log and spread inside of roll with 1½ cups of frosting. Reroll, but without the towel this time.

Use a spreader or butter knife.

8 Use remaining frosting to cover outside of cake. You can use a fork to make frosting look like tree bark.

If cake breaks while rolling, cover cracks with frosting.

ingredients...

For the cake:
18.25-oz (517-g) box vanilla cake mix
4 eggs
½ cup water
⅓ cup vegetable oil

For the filling and frosting:
2 12- to 16-oz (340- to 450-g) tubs of chocolate frosting
1 cup hazelnut-flavored spread

Note: you can decorate your cake any way you like. Try sprinkles or multi-colored icing.

This recipe is dairy. For a kosher meal, serve only with other dairy or pareve foods.

PURIM

Purim brings friends, feasts, and fanciful costumes together!
Get dressed up and host your own Purim festival. Enjoy
hamantaschen, kreplach, lentil salad, delicious deli sandwiches,
and more as you celebrate the bravery of Esther.

Kreplach are like little dumplings.

Purim honors the brave and beautiful
Esther and her Uncle Mordechai. Long
ago they protected the Jewish people
living in Persia from the evil Haman,
who hoped to destroy them. It is a
holiday that is both serious and silly,
and is all about turning normal customs
upside down.

On Purim, the Book of Esther, or
Megillat Esther (also known as the
Megillah), is read out loud from a scroll.
The story tells how King Achashverosh,
a Persian, chose Esther, a Jew, to be
his wife. As the new Queen of Persia,
Esther hid her religious beliefs, fearing
for her safety. But when Achashverosh's

"The reading of *Megillat Esther* is done with a lot of audience participation. We are told to erase the name of Haman so every time his name is read in the story, we make lots of noise to drown out the sound of his name." —Rabbi Ozur Bass

general, Haman, called for the deaths of all Jewish people in Persia, Esther bravely asked her husband the king to spare the lives of her people. With the help of her Uncle Mordechai, Esther turned a scary time for the Jewish people into a time of great celebration.

There are many different foods that are served on Purim, including delicious hamantaschen, which means "pockets of poppyseeds" in German. In Israel they are called "*oznei Haman*," or "Haman's ears."

Some people eat vegetarian feasts in honor of Esther, as it is said that Esther ate only seeds and nuts when she was living in the palace to make sure she followed the rules of kashrut.

Along with the delicious food come fun and festive Purim customs. People wear costumes and masks to the reading of *Megillat Esther*. What costumes do you wear for Purim?

Achashverosh's sandwich crown

This sandwich looks like a king's crown, and will feed a crowd. Everyone will get into the festive spirit of Purim!

get cooking...

1 Preheat oven to 350°F (180°C).

2 Roll dough into a snake 2 feet (60 cm) long and about 3 inches (7.5 cm) in diameter.

3 Place on greased baking sheet, forming a circle and pressing ends together. Brush bread with oil and sprinkle with sesame seeds.

4 Bake for 25 to 30 minutes, until golden brown.

5 Allow bread to cool, then have an adult slice the ring horizontally.

Ask an adult to slice the bread.

6 Layer lettuce, turkey, pastrami, tomatoes, and onions on bottom half of loaf.

Layer on as much as you want!

7 Spread mayonnaise and mustard on other half of loaf, and place on top.

8 To finish your crown sandwich, you can put a grape tomato and olive on each toothpick. Stick them into the loaf to resemble gems and jewels on a crown.

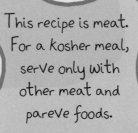

This recipe is meat. For a Kosher meal, serve only with other meat and pareve foods.

ingredients...

24 oz (680 g) bread dough

2 tablespoons vegetable oil

1 tablespoon sesame seeds

1 cup lettuce, shredded, or 10 leaves

½ pound (225 g) deli turkey

½ pound (225 g) deli pastrami

½ cup tomato, sliced

¼ cup red onion, thinly sliced

3 tablespoons mayonnaise

3 tablespoons yellow mustard

For serving:

10 toothpicks

10 grape tomatoes and/or 10 olives

"On Purim afternoon, there is the tradition of sharing a large festive meal, called a *Seudah* (pronounced seh-oo-DAH). The meal begins with people making jokes and creating funny versions of some of the traditional prayers said at more serious holiday meals."
— Rabbi Ozur Bass

You can use ready-made refrigerated bread loaves, defrosted store-bought dough, or challah dough.

"The Persian Jewish community celebrates Purim with big parties. One of my friends, whose parents are Iranian, gets together with many other Persian Jewish women. They each make their own version of sesame-seed candy and have taste tests."

—Rabbi Ozur Bass

Be careful: Sometimes small rocks can be mixed in with raw lentils.

Persian lentil salad

This recipe includes traditional Persian ingredients like mint, parsley, and lime juice. And because lentils are seeds (not beans), they represent the seeds that Esther ate to keep kosher while she lived at the palace.

ingredients...

½ cup dry lentils

2 cups water

1 teaspoon salt

1 cup chickpeas

1 cup green bell pepper, diced

1 cup red bell pepper, diced

1 cup yellow bell pepper, diced

1 tablespoon jalapeno pepper, minced

¼ cup green onion, chopped

¼ cup mint, chopped

¼ cup parsley, chopped

2 tablespoons lime juice

2 tablespoons olive oil

get cooking...

1 Cook lentils by bringing lentils, water, and salt to a boil. Reduce heat to medium and cook for 25 minutes or until lentils are tender. Drain and rinse with cold water.

2 Toss together cooked lentils and all other ingredients in a bowl. Serve warm or chilled.

This recipe is pareve. For a kosher meal, serve with either dairy or meat foods.

You can use canned lentils for this recipe:

Drain and rinse 1 15-oz (425-g) can of lentils and reduce cooking time to 15 to 20 minutes.

turkey kreplach

Kreplach are a traditional Jewish food any time, not just on Purim. Like the suspense of the Purim story, the contents of a kreplach remain a mystery until you bite into it! This recipe features a turkey filling, but you can use whatever meat or veggies you like.

get cooking...

1   Preheat oven to 375°F (190°C).

2   Combine all ingredients in a bowl except wrappers and oil.

3   Cut wonton wrappers in half using knife or pizza cutter. Wrappers should then be rectangles.

4   Place a teaspoon of mixture on wrapper and fold twice to form a triangle. On the final fold, moisten the edge of the wrapper with water to seal the dough.

5   Brush baking sheets with vegetable oil and place kreplach on them. Brush tops of kreplach with oil. Bake for 13 to 15 minutes. Kreplach should be crunchy and golden brown.

Fold the corner over to make a triangle.

ingredients...

1 pound (450 g) ground turkey, cooked

12 oz (340 g) spinach, cooked and chopped

1 egg

¾ cup bread crumbs

½ teaspoon garlic powder

1 teaspoon Italian spice mix (garlic, basil, and oregano)

3 tablespoons vegetable oil

1 package square egg roll or wonton wrappers

Note: Egg roll or wonton wrappers can be found in the produce section of most grocery stores.

Kreplach are very similar to Italian ravioli or Chinese wontons.

This recipe is meat. For a kosher meal, serve only with other meat or pareve foods.

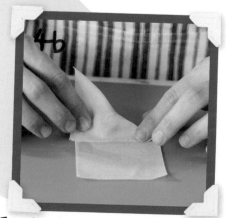

Fold the triangle across the wrapper for the second fold.

"Kreplach are a delicious addition to any good soup. Sometimes I take kreplach that I have frozen and put them in my Shabbat chicken soup."

-Rabbi Ozur Bass

Kreplach can also be cooked by boiling in broth or deep frying in oil.

hamantaschen

Hamantaschen are reminders of when Persian Jews were saved from Haman's cruelty. These cookies resemble the tri-cornered hat that evil Haman wore.

ingredients...

1½ cups butter, softened

1 cup sugar

2 eggs, beaten

3 tablespoons orange juice

½ teaspoon vanilla extract

½ teaspoon salt

2 teaspoons baking powder

5 cups all-purpose flour

½ cup apricot jam or preserves

½ cup raspberry jam or preserves

Note: a 3-inch (7.5-cm) round cookie cutter will work best, but if you don't have one then you can use a drinking glass of the same size.

Allow some jam to show through.

get cooking...

1 Beat butter and sugar together.

2 Combine eggs, orange juice, and vanilla in small bowl. Add to butter mixture and combine. Add salt and baking powder, then add flour 1 cup at a time until dough forms.

3 Refrigerate dough for at least 1 hour.

4 Preheat oven to 350°F (180°C). Line baking sheets with parchment paper.

5 Roll out dough until it is ¼ inch (½ cm) thick. Cut out circles using a cookie cutter or a glass, and place on parchment.

6 Put a scant teaspoon of preserves in center of each circle. Pinch sides of circles together to create a triangle. Place formed cookies in freezer for 10 minutes.

Try not to overload with jam.

7 Remove from freezer and bake for 10 to 12 minutes. Cookies should be slightly browned.

"Every year my sisters and I helped our mother make hamantaschen. We sang and laughed and had so much fun as we rolled and cut and filled and pinched. I know the cookies tasted better because we were smiling when we made them."
—Rabbi Ozur Bass

This recipe is dairy. For a kosher meal, serve only with other dairy or pareve foods.

Prune preserves are traditional, but you can use whatever flavor you like.

PESACH

Pesach brings families together to the seder table in celebration of their history and traditions. It is a time to remember the struggles of the Israelites, and to eat and enjoy matzoh, haroset, meringues, and other treats from the Old World.

Pesach, or Passover, celebrates the trials and triumphs of the Israelite people in Egypt.

Pharaoh kept the Israelites as slaves, and treated them cruelly for many years. When he finally decided to let the Israelites follow Moses out of Egypt, the Israelites left in a hurry because they feared that Pharaoh would change his mind. He did change his mind, and sent his army after them. So the Israelites fled into the desert.

Seder plate

Because they left Egypt so quickly, the Israelites did not have time to let their bread dough rise before baking it. So instead of having leavened bread, they had flat matzoh. To remember the escape of Israelite ancestors, many Jews do not eat leavened foods during Pesach. Some families completely remove anything that contains flour or leavening agents (called "*chametz*") from their homes during Pesach.

"The Torah teaches that the first seder was held the night before the Israelites left Egypt. They ate Passover lamb and talked about the miracles that were happening all around them."

—Rabbi Ozur Bass

During the first two nights of Pesach, a seder is held, at which the Haggadah is read aloud. *Haggadah* means "the telling," and it tells the story of the Israelites' flight from Egypt.

Everything on the seder table is used to help tell the story, especially the items placed on the special seder plate. The symbolic foods on the seder plate are: a roasted shank bone, a roasted egg, horseradish, romaine lettuce (or parsley), celery, and haroset.

After the Haggadah is read, families celebrate with a delicious, festive meal. Many of the dishes traditionally served hearken back to ancient times, and are based on the foods available to the Israelites as they continued their journey through the desert.

Meringue cookies are perfect for Pesach.

haroset

Much of the seder is about the bitterness and sorrow of life in Egypt under Pharaoh. While haroset (pronounced *ha-ROH-set*) looks like the mortar that the Israelites used to build Egyptian cities, it tastes sweet to celebrate being freed from Egypt. Here are two different ways to prepare it: Ashkenazic (which is not cooked) and Sephardic (which is).

Ashkenazic

ingredients...

For the Ashkenazic apple haroset:

6 apples, peeled, cored, and chopped

1 cup walnuts, finely chopped

½ teaspoon ground cinnamon

1 teaspoon sugar

1 tablespoon honey

⅓ cup grape juice

For the Sephardic haroset:

1 cup dried figs

1 cup dried dates, pitted

¾ cup raisins

¼ cup honey

¼ cup water

½ teaspoon cinnamon

¼ cup orange marmalade

½ cup walnuts, finely chopped

ashkenazic apple haroset:

1 Put all ingredients in bowl and mix, crushing apples slightly with spoon.

sephardic haroset:

1 Place all ingredients in saucepan over medium heat. Cook for 5 to 7 minutes or until marmalade melts and fruits are warmed through. Serve immediately.

Both of these recipes are pareve, and can be served with meat, dairy, or other pareve foods.

"Every Jewish community around the world has its own tradition of how to make haroset. Some are sweet, others are more tart or even spicy." —Rabbi Ozur Bass

Sephardic

You can add strips of orange peel to your haroset, for more flavor.

citrus salmon en papillote

serves 4

Eating fish is not that common on Passover, but it can be a nice change from the heavier foods that are traditionally served at the seder.

get cooking...

1 Preheat oven to 400°F (200°C). In a small bowl, mix olive oil, tarragon, garlic, orange peel, lemon peel, brown sugar, and orange juice.

2 Cut 4 squares of parchment paper, each 12 x 12 inches (30 x 30 cm). Place sliced onions in the center of each sheet of parchment.

3 Place a piece of salmon on each bed of onions. Spread each piece of salmon with orange peel mixture, then place an orange and lemon slice on top of each fillet.

Wash your hands after touching raw fish.

4 Pull all sides of parchment paper up to form a bundle. Tie with string so parchment paper looks like a small sack.

Tie the bundles tightly.

5 Place packets on baking sheet and bake for 17 to 20 minutes.

6 Ask an adult to cut open the packets (they'll be hot and steamy), and help put each salmon stack on a plate.

ingredients...

2 tablespoons olive oil

1 teaspoon fresh tarragon, minced

2 cloves garlic, minced

1 teaspoon orange peel

1 teaspoon lemon peel

1 teaspoon brown sugar

1 tablespoon orange juice

1 red onion, sliced into thin rings

4 4-oz (112-g) salmon fillets

4 orange slices

4 lemon slices

Note: Other citrus fruits, such as lime and grapefruit will also work well.

"There many different traditions, laws, and customs about food on Passover. Many of the customs depend on how the food was processed or prepared in different Jewish communities all over Europe, Africa, or Asia."
—Rabbi Ozur Bass

This recipe is pareve, so it may be served with either dairy or meat foods.

Steam will get trapped in the packet, and that's what cooks the salmon.

"Sephardic Jews and Jews from Northern Africa have big celebrations called 'Mimouna' as Passover is ending. They open their doors and serve mint tea and many wonderful foods to all the guests who can fit in their homes." —Rabbi Ozur Bass

savory mina

This Sephardic meat pie features ground beef, mashed potato, onions, and spices simmered in a hearty gravy and then baked in matzoh crust.

get cooking...

1 Preheat oven to 350°F (180°C).

2 Put beef, potato, onion, salt, pepper, cinnamon, allspice, and water in skillet. Simmer over medium heat for 30 minutes.

3 While meat mixture cooks, soak 4 matzoh sheets in warm water until they are very soft—almost mushy.

4 Squeeze moisture out of the wet matzoh using paper towels. Press matzoh onto bottom and sides of a 9-inch (23-cm) pie pan.

5 Brush matzoh with 1 tablespoon of vegetable oil and place in oven for 2 to 3 minutes.

6 After meat is finished cooking, spoon into matzoh crust.

7 Soak remaining matzoh in warm water until soft. Place pieces of softened matzoh on top of meat mixture to form an outer crust. When finished, brush with remaining vegetable oil and then bake for 20 minutes.

ingredients...

1 pound (450 g) ground beef

1 large potato, baked and mashed

½ cup onion, minced

½ teaspoon salt

½ teaspoon ground black pepper

½ teaspoon ground cinnamon

½ teaspoon ground allspice

1 cup water

8 matzoh sheets

1 to 2 cups warm water

2 tablespoons vegetable oil

This recipe is meat. For a kosher meal, serve only with other meat or pareve dishes.

Sephardic Jews are descended from Jews in Spain, Portugal, and Turkey.

pesach ★

93

froggy meringue cookies

Meringue cookies are often served at Passover because they do not use any flour or leavening agents. We've put a fun twist on ours: Instead of plain white meringues we're making frogs!

get cooking...

1 Preheat oven to 200°F (95°C). Line baking sheets with parchment paper.

2 Separate eggs by carefully cracking each egg into a bowl and then gently scooping out the yolk.

Be careful not to break the yolk.

Keep the yolks for another recipe.

3 Put egg whites in bowl. Use electric mixer to beat eggs until they are light and foamy.

4 Add sugar a little bit at a time. Eventually the mixture will become shiny and peaks will stand up when the beaters are removed. (Turn them off first!)

5 Put ½ cup of meringue into a pastry bag or sandwich bag and set aside.

6 Add vanilla and food coloring to rest of meringue mixture, and gently stir until color is even.

7 Drop a tablespoon of green meringue onto parchment paper for the frog's head. Then use pastry bag or plastic bag to add two white meringue dots. Push chocolate chips into dots to form eyeballs.

ingredients...

4 egg whites

2½ cups confectioners' (powdered) sugar

½ teaspoon vanilla extract

3 drops green food coloring

2 oz (56 g) mini chocolate chips

Note: If you do not have a pastry bag, you can snip the corner off of a plastic sandwich bag and use that instead. (Fill the bag before you snip!)

Make the eyes large or small!

Not into frogs? Omit food coloring and chocolate chips. By omitting chocolate chips, this recipe becomes pareve, not dairy.

pesach

94

"I love this recipe because we always have toy frogs all over our seder table. The frogs were one of 10 terrible plagues in Egypt that God sent to convince Pharaoh to let the Israelites out of slavery." —Rabbi Ozur Bass

This recipe is dairy. For a kosher meal, serve only with other dairy or pareve foods.

Use a glass or metal bowl to help your meringue stiffen properly.

matzoh brei

Matzoh brei (pronounced *MAHT-zoh BRY*) is a fun-to-eat breakfast. It's a lot like traditional French toast, only it's made with matzoh instead of bread.

ingredients...

1 sheet of matzoh

2 tablespoons hot water

1 egg

1 tablespoon butter or canola oil

cinnamon and sugar for topping

get cooking...

1 Break matzoh into small pieces and put in bowl with hot water.

2 In another bowl, beat the egg with a fork.

3 Melt butter or heat oil in frying pan over medium heat.

4 Pour egg over matzoh, then pour into hot pan.

5 Let mixture become golden brown. Flip and cook the other side to golden brown.

6 Sprinkle with cinnamon and sugar and serve immediately.

"We wait all year to eat matzoh brei! We like it for an easy lunch or dinner. After the heavy meals of the seder, it is good to eat lighter foods for the rest of the week of Passover."
—Rabbi Ozur Bass

This recipe is dairy. For a kosher meal, serve only with other dairy or pareve foods.

Matzoh brei can be made savory by adding onions, peppers, or mushrooms to the matzoh-and-egg mixture.

YOM HA'ATZMAUT

The flavors of Israel are celebrated on Israeli Independence Day. People gather at springtime barbecues to dance and sing *HaTikvah*, and eat hummus, falafel, baba ghanoush, *shakshouka* and more!

Yom Ha'Atzmaut is Israeli Independence Day. This day marks the birth of the modern State of Israel.

Yom Ha'Atzmaut is all about pride in Israel and celebrating with friends. It is also a day to feast on traditional Israeli foods, and to take in the beauty of the land by spending time outside. In Israel, many people enjoy barbecues and parties, where there is plenty of Israeli folk dancing and singing.

For Jewish people elswhere, observing Yom Ha'Atzmaut is a way to show support for the country of Israel. It is very much like Fourth-of-July festivities in the United States.

Why is celebrating Israel important? Because Israel is the homeland of the Jewish people. Although there are Jewish communities all around the world, a dedication to the land of Israel

Israeli flags fly high on Yom Ha'Atzmaut.

"You can make your barbecue extra festive with lots of blue and white decorations."

—Rabbi Ozur Bass

has held Jewish people together throughout time.

For almost two thousand years Jews lived without a land of their own. So when Israel finally became a modern state for the Jewish people—in 1948 — it was as if a great miracle had happened. Because of this, Yom Ha'Atzmaut is not just a political holiday, but a religious holiday, too.

The rejoicing and celebrating of Israeli Independence Day is a welcome time in spring, because people often gather at outdoor picnics and barbecues. It is especially welcome because it comes after solemn holidays, including

Yom Ha'Shoah, which is a day to remember all of the people who perished in the Holocaust.

No matter where you live, celebrating Yom Ha'Atzmaut is easy. The fresh spring fruits and vegetables on the menu can be found everywhere. And most supermarkets have Israeli products in their international foods section.

So get your pots and pans ready, it's time to cook and celebrate!

Israeli salad

serves
8

Simple foods can be delicious. This refreshing salad perks up every meal. It is great alongside eggs at breakfast, stuffed in a pita with falafel at lunch, or paired with roasted lamb at dinner.

ingredients...

2 cups cucumber, peeled, seeded, and diced

2 cups tomatoes, seeded, and diced

½ cup onion, fincely minced

3 tablespoons olive oil

2 tablespoons lemon juice

½ teaspoon salt

½ teaspoon *za'atar* (optional)

get cooking...

1 Combine all ingredients in a bowl and serve cold.

This recipe is pareve and can be served with dairy or meat recipes.

Za'atar is a strong Middle Eastern spice that tastes a little like oregano. It is actually a mixture of spices, much like curry. And also like curry, every spice seller in Israel has his or her own secret recipe for the mixture of spices in za'atar.

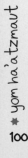

★ yom ha'atzmaut

"When I am in Israel, one of my favorite breakfasts is Israeli salad mixed with fresh yogurt and za'atar."
—Rabbi Ozur Bass

Israeli salad has many varieties. Experiment by adding different fresh spices like mint, parsley or dill.

baked falafel patties and hummus

Falafel and hummus are popular and traditional foods in Israel. Almost every street corner has a falafel shop just bursting with the flavors of the Middle East. Invite friends who have been to Israel to your Yom Ha'Atzmaut feast. Ask them about the sights, sounds, smells, and tastes of their journey.

falafel patties:

1 Preheat oven to 400°F (200°C).

2 Mash chickpeas in large bowl. Add onion, parsley, and garlic.

3 In a separate bowl, mix egg, olive oil, hot sauce, lemon juice, baking powder, cumin, coriander, and salt. Add to chickpea mixture and stir.

4 Add bread crumbs, using your hands to combine. If mixture is sticky, add more bread crumbs. If mixture is too dry to form patties, add more olive oil.

5 Form into 20 patties, each about 2 inches (5 cm) in diameter.

6 Place patties on lightly oiled baking sheet and bake for 15 minutes. Flip patties and bake for 15 more minutes.

hummus:

1 Place all ingredients except olive oil in blender or food processor, and blend until smooth.

2 If hummus is thicker than you like, stir in some olive oil.

3 Place hummus in bowl and serve with a drizzle of olive oil on top.

Falafel can also be deep fried.

Heat 1 cup vegetable oil in a large, heavy skillet over medium-high heat. Have an adult fry patties for 1 to 2 minutes per side or until golden brown.

ingredients...

For the falafel:

1 15-oz (425-g) can chickpeas, drained

½ cup onion, grated

½ cup parsley, finely minced

2 cloves garlic, finely minced

1 egg

2 tablespoons olive oil

2 teaspoons hot sauce (optional)

1 teaspoon lemon juice

1 teaspoon baking powder

1 teaspoon cumin

1 teaspoon coriander

½ teaspoon salt

1 cup bread crumbs

For the hummus:

1 15-oz (425-g) can chickpeas, drained

¼ cup sesame tahini

3 tablespoons lemon juice

1 clove garlic, crushed

½ teaspoon cumin

2 teaspoons olive oil

★ yom ha'atzmaut

"A good falafel seller in Israel makes quite a show when putting the falafel into the pita. Like a pizza maker, he will toss the balls into the air with his tongs and catch them in the pita!"   –Rabbi Ozur Bass

These recipes are pareve and can be served with dairy or meat meals.

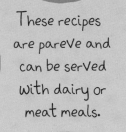

A warm pita stuffed with delicious falafel, hummus, and Israeli salad is a healthy and tasty lunch.

If you like spicy food, you can add some chopped jalapeños, too.

shakshouka

Meaning "all mixed up" in Hebrew, *shakshouka* is a traditional Sephardic breakfast. The eggs poach in the tomatoey sauce, and it's all served out of the same pan.

ingredients...

2 tablespoons olive oil

2 cloves garlic, crushed

½ cup onion, chopped

2 cups tomatoes, cubed

1 cup green peppers, chopped

1 cup red peppers, chopped

4 eggs

⅛ teaspoon red chili flakes (optional)

This recipe is pareve, and can be served with dairy or meat foods.

get cooking...

1 Heat oil in a nonstick frying pan over medium-high heat, then add garlic and onion. Cook until tender, 4 to 5 minutes.

2 Add tomatoes and peppers. After a few minutes, turn heat down to medium. Allow mixture to simmer for 20 minutes.

3 Create 4 wells in the tomato mixture, each about the size of an egg.

4 Carefully crack an egg into small bowl. Pour into well. Repeat until you have 4 eggs cooking. Place lid on pan and turn heat to low. Cook until eggs are as firm as you like. Sprinkle chili flakes over *shakshouka* before serving.

"In a traditional kosher home, eggs can be used only if they have no spots on the yolks. We crack the egg carefully into a glass, inspect it, and then put it into the bowl. Cracking and checking the eggs is a great way to include younger children." —Rabbi Ozur Bass

yom ha'atzmaut ★ 105

baba ghanoush

A taste of the Middle East, this is a healthy snack to eat anytime with pita, crackers, and cut-up vegetables.

get cooking...

1 Preheat oven to 400°F (200°C). Wash the eggplant and prick its skin several times with a fork. Place on a baking sheet and roast in oven for 45 minutes. Remove from oven and let cool.

2 Once cool, scrape roasted eggplant (seeds and all) from its skin into bowl.

A spoon works great for this.

3 Put eggplant, lemon juice, tahini, olive oil, garlic, and salt into food processor. Process until the mixture becomes smooth.

4 Sprinkle with paprika and serve.

ingredients...

1 medium eggplant

¼ cup lemon juice

¼ cup sesame tahini

2 tablespoons olive oil

2 cloves garlic, fincely minced

¼ teaspoon salt

¼ teaspoon paprika

Note: Tahini can be found in natural food stores or the Middle Eastern foods section of large grocery stores.

Tahini is easy to make from scratch.

Put 1 cup of sesame seeds in the food processor with ⅓ cup of vegetable oil. Process until seeds are broken down and mixture is smooth.

This recipe is pareve, and can be served with either dairy or meat foods.

"Eggplants are found in cuisine from all over the Mediterranean region, especially in many Italian Jewish recipes."

–Rabbi Ozur Bass

LAG B'OMER

Hot sunny days and breezy warm nights are the perfect occasion for Lag B'Omer celebrations. Enjoy the season with kebabs, fresh salads, and icy-cold, refreshing pomegranate lemonade!

Pomegranate-seed ice cubes are a nice touch!

Lag B'Omer is the thirty-third day of the counting of the omer. The omer are the 49 days between Pesach and Shavuot.

The word *omer* means "sheaf." A sheaf is a bundle of grain. During the 49 days of the omer ancient Jewish people would celebrate the first crop—the barley crop—being harvested. In ancient Israel they would cut measures of barley for each of the 49 days and bring them to the Temple as an offering to God.

Today, the Jewish people still count these days in anticipation of Shavuot, which honors the gift of the Torah from God.

"Lag is not really a word. It is a combination of the Hebrew letters that form the number 33. It stands for the thirty-third day of the counting of the omer."   —Rabbi Ozur Bass

The counting of the omer is a serious time, and many people believe that certain activities and celebrations, like weddings and parties—even getting a haircut—are forbidden during this time.

However, the thirty-third day of the count—Lag B'Omer—is for rejoicing. Many weddings occur on this day, as well as school festivals, parties, picnics, and bonfires. Athletic events and archery competitions are also associated with Lag B'Omer, in recognition of a brief military victory in ancient Israel.

This holiday falls when the weather is getting warmer, which makes the parties and picnics that much more fun.

Sporting events and big parties feel extra special when the sun is shining!

Celebrate Lag B'Omer with seasonal fruits, fresh vegetables, and dishes that are perfect for barbecues and picnics.

tabbouleh

Refreshing but zesty, this cracked-wheat salad is great to eat at barbecues, or for a quick lunch on Shabbat. Use crisp romaine lettuce leaves as spoons to eat your tabbouleh.

get cooking...

1 Have an adult pour boiling water over bulgur wheat and cover the bowl with plastic wrap. Set aside for 1 hour. Drain and let cool.

2 In same bowl, mix together all ingredients except lettuce.

3 Serve your room-temperature (or chilled) salad on lettuce leaves.

This recipe is pareve and can be served with dairy or meat dishes.

ingredients...

½ cup boiling water

¼ cup bulgur wheat

2½ cups tomatoes, seeded and diced

½ cup scallions, sliced

1 cup cucumber, seeded and diced

1 cup fresh parsley, chopped

¼ cup fresh mint, chopped

2 tablespoons lemon juice

2 tablespoons olive oil

2 teaspoons salt

⅛ teaspoon allspice

8 leaves Romaine lettuce

Bulgur wheat tastes nutty.

"Tabbouleh is often served as a side salad. I like mine on a hot summer day with a lot of extra lemon." -Rabbi Ozur Bass

Tabbouleh can be spelled many ways, such as taboule, tabboleh, tabouleh, and tabuli.

lamb and Vegetable shish kebabs

Tender meat and juicy vegetables are made even more flavorful after being grilled over an open flame for a true taste of the Middle East.

ingredients...

For the marinade:

2 cloves garlic, crushed

3 tablespoons lemon juice

¼ cup canola oil

¼ cup fresh parsley, chopped

1 teaspoon coriander

1 teaspoon cumin

For the kebabs:

1 pound (450 g) lamb fillet, cut into 20 1-inch (2.5-cm) cubes

1 green pepper, cut into 12 chunks

12 cherry tomatoes

Note: you can use metal or bamboo skewers for this recipe.

pomegranate lemonade

Taste Israel's sunshine in your glass. This is more tart and tangy than plain lemonade.

ingredients
6 lemons
5 cups cold water
1 cup pomegranate juice
1 cup sugar

1. Juice lemons. (Be sure to pick out all the seeds.)

2. Combine lemon juice, water, pomegranate juice, and sugar in pitcher. Stir well. Serve chilled.

get cooking...

1 Whisk together marinade ingredients. Pour over lamb chunks and refrigerate for at least 2 hours.

2 Assemble kabobs by alternating meat chunks and vegetables on skewers.

3 Have an adult place skewers on heated grill. Cook for 5 minutes and flip over, then cook until done, about 5 more minutes.

This recipe is meat. To plan a kosher meal, serve only with other meat or pareve foods.

You can also broil the kebabs.

Lag b'omer

watermelon salad

Juicy watermelon, succulent tomatoes, crunchy celery, and tasty onion come together in a refreshing salad that is perfect for barbecues. Hollow out the watermelon halves carefully and you can use them as serving bowls.

ingredients...

¼ cup red wine vinegar

2 teaspoons sugar

2 cups watermelon, seeded and diced

1 cup tomatoes, seeded and diced

¼ cup celery, diced

¼ cup red onion, minced

This recipe is pareve and may be served with meat or dairy for a kosher meal.

get cooking...

1 In a bowl, combine red wine vinegar and sugar.

2 Add all other ingredients to bowl and toss to coat with liquid. Serve chilled.

Be creative! Use cookie cutters to cut out watermelon shapes to garnish your salad. Or make an ice bowl in which to serve your salad. Be careful, though—ice bowls don't last very long at picnics!

Watermelon is a great source of vitamins A and C.

"Watermelons are abundant in Israel during the summer months. Because of this, they're always part of an Israeli picnic, especially one celebrating Lag B'Omer."

—Rabbi Ozur Bass

SHAVUOT

Delicious dairy foods are traditional on Shavuot. Friends and family gather to celebrate the presentation of the Torah, and then spend hours in discussion and debate. Refresh with creamy cheesecake, blintzes, and stuffed French toast.

The word *Shavuot* means "weeks" in Hebrew. This holiday occurs at the conclusion of the seven-week counting of the omer. These seven weeks correspond to when the first barley crop was harvested in ancient times. The end of the omer is Shavuot, which marks the beginning of the main harvest season. Shavuot also commemorates God's giving the Torah to the Jewish people. The Torah is the central text of the Jewish people, and is the foundation of Jewish identity and law. It is a sacred text, and so Jewish people rejoice on Shavuot.

There are many customs attached to Jewish holidays, and on Shavuot, there is a custom to eat dairy foods. No one really knows where this custom comes from, and people give many different reasons.

One idea is that when the Israelites received the Torah, God reminded them of the promise to lead them to "a land of milk and honey." As a reminder of this promise, the first meal eaten on Shavuot features dairy foods, such as

"In ancient times the first fruits of the season, called *bikkurim*, were brought to the Temple in Jerusalem as an offering to God."

—Rabbi Ozur Bass

cheesecake, blintzes, and ice cream.

Shavuot falls when trees and fields are flowering, so decorating with flowers and eating fresh seasonal fruits are also traditional.

The most interesting Shavuot tradition is to stay up all night with friends and family, studying the Torah. There are always lively discussions and debates about history and culture, and wonderful memories are made. This is called a *Tikun Leil Shavuot*.

Will you stay up all night next Shavuot? If you do, be sure to bring some of these delicious treats to your party!

Top your French toast with powdered sugar.

stuffed French toast

serves
4

Everyone will be delighted by the taste of red, ripe strawberries bursting from this French toast filling. Strawberries are a sweet part of the spring harvest!

get cooking...

1 Whisk eggs, milk, vanilla, and cinnamon together in a shallow bowl. Set aside.

2 Divide strawberry cream cheese among four slices of bread and spread evenly to the edges. Place remaining 4 slices on top to make 4 sandwiches.

3 Heat 1 tablespoon of butter in frying pan over medium heat.

4 Dip one sandwich in the egg mixture and coat it entirely on both sides. Place in pan and cook until golden. Flip and cook until other side is golden. Repeat with remaining butter and sandwiches.

5 When cooked sandwiches have cooled a bit, use cookie cutters to make French toast shapes!

ingredients...

2 eggs

⅔ cup milk

1 teaspoon vanilla extract

½ teaspoon cinnamon

About 4 oz (112 g) strawberry cream cheese, at room temperature (see page 46 for recipe)

8 slices of bread (challah works great!)

4 tablespoons butter

Note: use any flavor cream cheese you like.

This recipe is dairy. For a kosher meal, serve only with other dairy or pareve foods.

"When I was young, my family used to go strawberry picking every year and we always came home with very full bellies and baskets. To me, the summer still can't start without spending time with my family in the strawberry fields!"
—Rabbi Ozur Bass

5a

Watch out for hot cream cheese!

5b

Use any shapes you want!

French toast tastes great with maple syrup and powdered sugar.

If you like your French toast eggy and rich, allow bread to absorb more mixture.

"No one really knows why we eat dairy on Shavuot. My favorite reason is because we say that the Torah is like milk and honey in our mouths. Just like milk helps us grow and keeps our bodies strong, the Torah helps our minds and souls grow and keeps our communities and families strong." —Rabbi Ozur Bass

Blintzes are delicious topped with a dollop of sour cream or whipped cream.

blueberry blintzes

Blintzes are pancake-like crepes filled with creamy sweet cheeses. When smothered in blueberry sauce, there is no tastier way to celebrate Shavuot.

get cooking...

1 Preheat oven to 350°F (180°C).

2 Combine all blintz ingredients in bowl except crepes. Spread ¼ cup of mixture down middle of each crepe. Roll crepe and tuck ends in, burrito-style. Place blintzes seam-side down in 8-inch (20-cm) square baking dish.

3 Bake for 10 to 12 minutes or until warmed through.

Fold the sides in as you roll.

4 Combine blueberries, sugar, and cornstarch in small bowl. Microwave for 2 minutes and stir. Microwave for 2 more minutes and stir again, then pour over baked blintzes and serve.

ingredients...

For the blintzes:

1 cup small-curd cottage cheese

1 cup cream cheese, softened

½ cup powdered sugar

1 teaspoon vanilla extract

8 crepes, 8 inches (20 cm) in diameter

Note: Premade crepes can be found in the refrigerated case in the produce section of most grocery stores.

For the blueberry topping:

2 cups frozen blueberries

1 tablespoon sugar

1 teaspoon cornstarch

This recipe is dairy. For a kosher meal, serve only with other dairy or pareve foods.

shavuot

121

classic cheesecake

This cheesecake is so good that your family will ask you to make it for every holiday! You can experiment by adding mix-ins like chopped-up cookies or candy bars.

get cooking...

1 Preheat oven to 350°F (180°C). Grease a 9-inch (23-cm) springform pan thoroughly. Be sure to get the bottom edges of the pan.

2 In small bowl, mix crushed cookies and melted butter together until the mixture looks like wet sand. Spoon into bottom of springform pan and press down to form crust.

3 In medium bowl, mix cream cheese and sugar until just combined. Add milk and vanilla, stirring gently. Then, gradually add beaten eggs.

4 Mix in sour cream and flour. If adding mix-ins, stir in gently.

5 Pour mixture into springform pan. Tap pan on countertop to remove air bubbles.

6 Bake for 60 minutes. Do not open the oven door at all, as cheesecake can crack.

7 After 60 minutes, turn oven off, even if cheesecake seems loose in the middle. Leave cheesecake to cool in oven with the door closed for 4 to 5 hours.

8 Refrigerate until served.

ingredients...

For the crust:
25 vanilla wafer cookies, crushed
4 tablespoons butter, melted

For the cheesecake:
2 pounds (900 g) cream cheese, at room temperature
1½ cups sugar
¾ cup milk
1 tablespoon vanilla extract
4 eggs, beaten
1 cup sour cream
3 tablespoons all-purpose flour

Optional:
½ cup mix-ins (such as chocolate chips, crushed cookies, crushed candy bars, broken-up brownies, fudge, peanut butter, or anything else you like)

"On Shavuot there is a tradition to stay up all night with people in the community learning and sharing thoughts about the Torah. Cheesecake is one of the most popular desserts on Shavuot because of the tradition to eat dairy. But I like it because the sugar helps me stay up late!"
–Rabbi Ozur Bass

Ingredients should always be at room temperature when you start.

This recipe is dairy. For a kosher meal, serve only with other dairy or pareve foods.

To crush cookies, place them in a sealed plastic bag and crush away!

To make this kosher for Passover, simply omit the flour and the cookie crust.

NOTES:

Jot down any notes, thoughts, or ideas that you have about any of the recipes in the book. When you make the recipes again, be sure to check back here to see your comments. This will help you add your personal flair to each dish!

NOTES:

INDEX

acknowledgments

Author's note:

Thanks to all who tried my recipes and washed my dishes. Special thanks to all my kids at the Charles E. Smith Jewish Day School, who taught me as much as I taught them. Very special thanks to Brian Bloomfield: *Ani L'Dodi V'Dodi Li.* Additional thanks to DK for believing in the value of teaching kids to cook, and for producing such beautiful books to that end. www.teachkidstocook.com

Publisher's note:

DK Publishing would like to thank the many people who made this book so delicious: Angela Coppola and assistants Ghazalle Badiozamani and Alfredo Fernandez; Susan Vajaranant and assistants Noura AlSalem, Matt Burdi, Rebecca Jurkevich, and Tracy Keshani; Josefina Munroe; Tamami Mihara; Liza Kaplan; Eugene Brophy; and Lorraine McCafferty. And especially our models: Andrew Cook, William Cook, Sydney Elizabeth, Allie Roth, David Roth, Daniel Schwabinger, Jake Schwabinger, Rowena Spector, Saskia Spector, Atalya Sternoff, Mia Sternoff, and Lauren Tomaselli.

Thank you to the Kaplan family, and Peggy and Mickey Knox for generously lending their knowledge and Judaica.

A very special thanks goes to the Charles Schiller Studio. www.studio-a-nyc.com

Photo credits:

Page 98: Israeli flag, Getty Images

Author Jill Colella Bloomfield is the founder of Picky Eaters, a kids' cooking consulting company. Along with creating materials for corporations about kids' cooking, she enjoys giving hands-on cooking lessons for kids aged two to teen. A devoted foodie, Jill loves adventures, such as touring farms and visiting food factories. Jill lives in St. Paul, Minnesota, and loves exploring the farmer's markets there.

Consultant Janet Ozur Bass is a Conservative Rabbi who teaches middle schoolers in Maryland. She loves cooking, reading, traveling, and hosting tons of people for every Jewish holiday and occassion she can think of. She has even been known to invent a few just to have an excuse to open her home. Janet is married to a cantor, and they are the proud parents of three terrific children.

Have fun while you cook!